Praise for *T*

"Having been invol... ... ... adult life I appreciated the political 'pearls of wisdom' contained in this book. It is the day-to-day actions that often impact people more than the big projects. Autry's book is a reminder of the many unsung heroes making a real difference in people's daily lives, as well as the value of second chances."
—Hon. Thomas Vilsack, Former Governor of Iowa, and US Secretary of Agriculture

"In James Autry's most recent book, *The White Man Who Stayed*, each chapter, each page and every word spoken takes us inside the homes and conversations of southern whites whose birth world of white dominance was disintegrating before them. James masterfully and honestly opens up the archives of his own mind where stored were private sightings and conversations remembered. In this biography, Autry brings to life, the personal journey of his own cousin who struggled to find his pathway in the only world he knew—the changing South. Unlike young Autry who left the South, his cousin took a deep breath, squared his shoulders and stayed behind."
—Clifton L. Taulbert, Pulitzer-nominated author, *The Last Train North, The Invitation, Once Upon A Time When We Were Colored*

"This profile in courage reminds us that no matter how ordinary we are, we can choose to stand for what is right. Douglas Autry did, leading Jim Autry to inspire us all through this marvelous story."
—Betty Sue Flowers, Former Director, Lyndon B. Johnson Presidential Library

"*The White Man Who Stayed* is a deeply touching memoir about a large-hearted man who acted with righteousness in a Mississippi still mired in its racial delusions. James Autry also brings to life a whole pre- and post-civil rights society, acting as a kind of Faulkner clarified, and giving us the context for his cousin Douglas Autry's bravery and compassion toward blacks and whites alike."
—Stephen Mitchell, translator of the *Tao Te Ching*

"This is an inspiring story about a man who lived through the racial conflicts of rural Mississippi, taking unpopular stands and working to help poor, under-educated African-Americans find their way. Douglas Autry is an unsung hero who finally gets his due through a memoir/biography written by his cousin, James Autry, one of our country's best writers."
—Charles Overby, Chairman of the Overby Center for Southern Journalism and Politics at Ole Miss

"With catalytic focus on racial injustice this timely book *The White Man Who Stayed* provides personal insight into the courageous journey of one man who stood up for equality and stood against hate, subjugation and the Southern Way of Life."
—Drake Sadler, Co-Founder of Traditional Medicinals

"*The White Man Who Stayed* is the author's personal tribute to Douglas Autry, a school superintendent in rural Benton County, Mississippi, who devoted his life to helping African-Americans. James Autry praises his cousin Douglas as a rare example of unselfish, courageous public service in a white-dominated closed society and credits him as an important influence in his state and beyond. Douglas Autry's dedicated service can be summed up in three words: Black Lives Matter. This is the kind of book we need right now."
—Lawrence Wells, author of *In Faulkner's Shadow: A Memoir.*

THE WHITE MAN
MAN
WHO STAYED

A Biography Remembered

James A. Autry

Ice Cube Press, LLC
North Liberty, Iowa USA

The White Man Who Stayed

Copyright ©2020 James A. Autry
Foreword © 2020 Bill Moyers

First Edition

Isbn 9781948509176

Library of Congress Control Number: 2020937443

Ice Cube Press, LLC (Est. 1991)
1180 Hauer Drive
North Liberty, Iowa 52317 USA
www.icecubepress.com | steve@icecubepress.com

The paper used in this publication meets the minimum
requirements of the American National Standard
for Information Sciences—Permanence of Paper for
Printed Library Materials, ANSI Z39.48-1992.

Manufactured in USA

DEDICATION

In memory of Harold Douglas Autry,
I dedicate this book to his wife Elizabeth,
his daughter Becky, and his sister Mary Jane.

FOREWORD
BY BILL MOYERS

There are Heroes, and there are heroes. The first are etched on the Mount Rushmores of our memory; their legacy, the dazzling triumph of courage over fear. The others, having shown us the character of persistence in ordinary life, fade quietly and anonymously into the past. In America's civil rights movement, the ground on which iconic heroes took their stand—the Martin Luther Kings and Rosa Parks, the Fannie Lou Hamers, James Farmers and Medgar Evers—would likely have hardened and grown fallow again had it not been tilled and hoed and harrowed by everyday heroism from the likes of Douglas Autry, whose story you are about to read.

Before beginning, however, consider how bad it was. The South, I mean. Not just the South of the Confederacy traumatized by its catastrophic defeat in the Civil War that it had waged to save slavery and white supremacy, but the South that rose again, resisted and routed Reconstruction—the Federal government's effort to bring freed slaves into full citizenship – and set about to resubjugate black people and restore white rule as "The Southern Way of Life."

Through the last quarter of the 19th century and well into the 20th, white extremism spread across the eleven states of the Old Confederacy. Politics thrived on bashing "nig-ras" and "niggers"—demeaning terms suggesting something less than human; as late as 1964 Lyndon Johnson of Texas, who was born into this culture shortly after the turn of the century and lived to challenge it at President, famously described how Southern politicians won and kept power by running against "nigger, nigger, nigger" as the ubiquitous scapegoat of white bigotry and fear. Across the South laws were passed to isolate black people and cement white superiority. Black judges? None. Black lawyers? Few. Severe restrictions on black people serving as plaintiffs, witnesses, and jurors? Many. Black doctors and nurses were forbidden to practice in white hospitals. Interracial dating: forbidden. Interracial marriages: Forbidden. Segregation ruled the parks, theatres, restaurants, libraries, schools, churches, water fountains and toilets. It even governed the grave: Cemeteries were white or black but never both.

How bad was it? Bad enough to inspire Nazi lawyers in Germany. They saw Germany with a "Jewish problem" similar to America's "Negro problem." If something weren't done, Jews might take over the country. Adolf Hitler already thought of America as a ripe utopia for the white race. In his polemic *Mein Kampf* he not only expressed admiration for America's commitment to racial purity, he praised the genocidal assaults that had "gunned down the millions of Redskins to a few hundred thousands." An influential German scholar called the founding of America a "fateful turning point" in the rise of Aryans. Without America, he wrote, "a conscious unity of the white race would never have emerged." Furthermore, the Americans had taken "great pains to guarantee that the decisive positions in the leadership of the state would be kept in the hands of Anglo-Saxons alone." Nazi lawyers found that enticing.

On June 5, 1934—the very day I was born—Adolph Hitler's top legal experts met to begin drawing up the infamous Nuremberg Laws that would embody the full-scale creation of a racist state, eventually legalizing the persecution and elimination of "undesirable" races (A stenographer produced verbatim transcripts of that meeting and others that followed over coming months.) Hitler's minister of justice began the first session by presenting a memorandum that laid out in detail laws adopted by American states to uphold white supremacy. Not only had Jim Crow laws caged black Americans into second-class citizenship, those laws were seen as models for the creation of a one-party system of racial purity very similar to what was emerging in fascist Europe. As the Nazis lawyers continued their work they showed sustained, serious, and prolonged interest in American race policies. The most radical among them were strongly in favor of using the American models in fulfilling Hitler's vision of the Third Reich. Ironically, they spurned certain US precedents as too harsh and rejected them. *Too harsh!* Still, our race laws were so indelibly linked to the shaping of Nazi policies that by the mid-1930s Germany and the American South had the look of a mirror image.

How bad was it? In his sweeping history of the generation just before the civil rights movement, *Speak Now Against the Day,* the late journalist John Egerton —Georgia-born and Tennessee-dwelling—describes how the violence employed to enforce Jim Crow segregation led to unbelievable cruelty, epitomized by the reality that victims of lynching "almost always died slow, agonizing, tortured deaths" from hanging, burning, beating, butchery, and other sadistic means. As blood streamed into the soil and soul of the South, the ever-tightening white code of racial conduct demanded increased conformity of thought and behavior. Anyone who questioned the racial status quo risked their livelihood and their life. They might wake up at night with a cross burning on their lawn, or be smeared as a Communist sympathizer, shunned by neighbors, and cold-shouldered at church.

No part of the South fought for white supremacy with more virulent ferocity than Mississippi, or was more effective in the use of intimidation, coercion, and threats. We learned more about this some 20 years ago when, after decades of court battles, Mississippi was ordered to open the secret files of the State Sovereignty Commission. The SSC was an official government agency, bountifully funded with taxpayer money, lavished with almost unlimited police and investigative powers, and charged with upholding segregation of the races. Most of the Southern states had similar agencies, but Mississippi had a well-deserved reputation as the worst.

At the time I reviewed some of those Sovereignty Commission files. As one longtime local advocate for justice in Jackson told a reporter: "They betray the absolute paranoia and craziness of the government in those times. This was a police state." And so it was.

The commission devoted astonishing amounts of effort, time, and money to snoop into the private lives of any citizen who supported civil rights, who *might* be supporting civil rights, or whom they suspected of stepping over the color line in any way. Its agents tracked down rumors that *this* volunteer from the north had venereal disease and *that one* was gay. They combed through letters to the editor in local and national newspapers and wrote outraged responses to anyone who criticized white supremacy. They went to concerts at black colleges to count how many white people were present, and posted spies at NAACP meetings to write down the license numbers of every car in the parking lot. They rummaged through the trash of suspected sympathizers of civil rights and paid undercover informants to report on leadership squabbles and whether white women were fornicating with black men. They even investigated a divorced mother of two after hearing rumors that her third child was fathered by a black man. When the agent sent to investigate first saw the child, he said "I had a weak feeling in the pit of my stomach." He and the sheriff acknowledged they were "not qualified to say it was a part Negro child but we could say it was not 100 percent Caucasian." The state then removed the mother's two older boys from her custody.

Reading those files I was struck by the brutality and banality of evil. A local legislator reported to the commission that a married white woman had given birth to a baby girl with "a mulatto complexion, dark hair that has a tendency to 'kink,' dark hands, and light palms." A doctor and investigator were dispatched to examine the child and determine paternity. The tests came back inconclusive, but a couple of months later shots were fired at night into the family's home and a threatening letter signed by the KKK, referring to "your wife and Negro child," was left on their doorstep. They moved out immediately.

Police state, yes, but this was also civil war by another name: Terrorism. It had long been employed to keep black people from voting. In 1946, for example, when Gene Talmadge was elected governor of Georgia on a frankly, even joyfully, racist platform, he said: "If I get a Negro vote it will be an accident." His machine figured out ways to challenge and purge the rolls. In Mississippi, the flambuoyant bigot Theodore Bilbo was reelected to the US Senate with the help of a campaign of threats and violence that kept most black people home on Election Day. "The way to keep the nigger from the polls is to see him the night before," Bilbo was fond of saying.

When the US Supreme Court ruled in 1954 that segregated schools were unconstitutional, the terrorists doubled down in their defense of white supremacy. Mississippi set the pace. The editor of the *Jackson*

Daily News, published in the capitol, drew a line that metaphorically connected the old Confederacy from Virginia to Texas. He put a black border around his front-page editorial entitled "Blood on the White Marble Steps" and declared, "This is a fight for white supremacy...there will be no room for neutrals or non-combatants....If you are a member of the Caucasian race....You are For Us or Against Us."

Douglas Autry had already decided which side he was for. He was born in 1926 when the South was still a feudal land plagued by boll weevils that left King Cotton dethroned and dying in the fields. The Depression of the 30s drove a demoralized people from their denuded farms in search of food, shelter, and work. Doug's family was luckier than others; his father owned enough Mississippi red dirt to scratch out a living, teach school, and serve several terms in the state legislature. His son went off to war in the Pacific when he was 17, then to college out of the state, and back home again to Mississippi where he remained until his death in 1996. Somewhere along the way, early on, while the majority of white neighbors lived in benign ignorance, apathy, or hostility toward black people down the road, Doug Autry quietly committed himself to working locally for the racial equality so long sought by the civil rights struggle. It still isn't exactly clear how he reached that decision in the midst of so much tumult in a state that boasted of its vicious resistance to justice, but he chose to stay. That's the thing: He stayed, and persisted.

I met him only once—at the Pine Grove Baptist Church, in Benton County, Mississippi. I was producing a PBS program about Doug's cousin Jim Autry, a fellow journalist, close friend, and the author of this book. Jim grew up nearby, but after graduating from Old Miss he left the South and distinguished himself at many endeavors, from fighter pilot to magazine publishing, from business and civic leadership to writing. By the time I went down with my film crew, Jim's poetry was gaining national recognition, and I wanted to meet his family and friends and learn of the experiences that had shaped him.

His cousin Doug came to the church that afternoon. I still remember the slight but firm twist of my wrist as he shook my hand. I can still see him sitting on the second row of the pews to my right; can still see how his eyes crinkled and the lines in his weathered face creased more deeply as the afternoon wore on. We didn't have much time to talk, but it wasn't talk that distinguished Doug Autry; it was presence.

There were others like him across the South. In time, there were many. They stayed for the hard, slow, stubborn work of integration. Sometimes they were successful, sometimes not. It is impossible to overstate the importance of their courage and persistence. So read this book slowly and carefully. It contains a slice of life which under Jim Autry's finely honed microscope reveals a universe of reality.

And if you still wonder why Doug Autry stood his ground, he just might have read *Macbeth*. For there it is written: "Screw your courage to the sticking-place/And we'll not fail."

Bill Moyers is an American journalist and political commentator. He served as White House Press Secretary under the Johnson administration from 1965 to 1967. He also worked as a network TV news commentator for ten years. Moyers has been extensively involved with public broadcasting, producing documentaries, and news journal programs. He has won numerous awards and honorary degrees for his investigative journalism and civic activities. He has become well-known as a trenchant critic of the corporately structured US news media.

PREFACE

~

I wrote the first version of this manuscript almost twenty years ago but could find no publisher interested in it. I was told that this story had already been told in one form or another. While I disagreed, I finally accepted that explanation, printed out a few copies of the manuscript for the family, then put it aside.

Early last year when it became apparent that racism was being not only tolerated but even encouraged by people of power and influence. I decided it might be time to try again to get the manuscript published.

Thus here it is.

The story is true though mostly long forgotten. All the characters are real, though most of them are now deceased. Also, many events from years ago are described as if they had recently happened. That's because the manuscript was written thirty years ago, then put aside.

I call this a biography remembered because it is simply that. In addition to Douglas Autry's family, I depended on the memories of people who either were directly part of the story or were simply part of the Benton County, Mississippi, community in which the events mostly took place.

While the hero of this story is Douglas, there were many heroes, not only white friends and family but most notably Douglas' African American staff plus parents and children of Benton County who not only supported Douglas but who faced daily taunts and threats from racist white people.

I recorded all the interviews with the exception of whose with close family members. The tapes are housed as part of my personal archives at the University of Mississippi.

JAA
September 1, 2019

CHAPTER ONE

~

I can make this quick. The facts are simple enough: country boy goes to war, comes home changed, goes to college, moves back to Mississippi home county, wins election as superintendent of education, makes political enemies, makes naïve mistakes, gets set up, tried and convicted to seven years in Mississippi's Parchman Farm, sentence suspended after 18 months, returns home, later goes to work in a federal program to help black and poor white people, endures harassment and cross-burnings by the Klan, is supported by black community and once again elected to superintendent of education, endures more harassment while overseeing school integration, retires and dies.

But as my Cousin Douglas always said, "Faulkner wasn't making anything up; he was just reporting it." Which means no one person's story begins and ends with him; it starts generations before, and in the South that means everyone's story is somehow connected to the Civil War or as we preferred to call it, The War Between The States. There are those in Mississippi who still refer to it as the War of Northern Aggression.

Our family had only one war story: It is told that my great great grandfather Jacob Autry rode with General Nathan Bedford Forrest who was reputed to be a superb military strategist whose techniques were studied by Nazi Field Marshall Erwin Rommel. (That connection has always intrigued me because Forrest also founded the Ku Klux Klan, as Nazi an organization as ever existed in this country and an organization that plays a small role in Cousin Douglas' story.)

In our family, we learned from early childhood that great great grandfather Jacob was shot off his horse during a skirmish near the Tennessee/Mississippi state line. A Yankee musket ball creased his forehead horizontally, making a bloody but superficial wound. He was knocked unconscious, however, and left for dead.

When he woke, his horse was gone, so he made what I consider one of the more rational and intelligent decisions ever made by an Autry: he just walked on home and quit the war altogether. The only evidence I have that this story is true is a photograph of a family setting in which great great grandfather Jacob has what appears to be a black horizontal streak across his forehead. I saw the photograph only once.

In one way or another, every Southerner's story is tied to that war and to race. Douglas' story is no different from mine except in one important way: Douglas stayed. I and many of my white Southern friends left the South not only to make our way in the cities of the North but—and this must be admitted—to leave behind the hard job we knew was coming, of finally integrating the South and bringing it into the 20th century. We knew it would be not only hard but bloody, probably very bloody.

As editor of the student newspaper at the University of Mississippi in the early fifties, I'd had a foretaste of the troubles to come when I published anything that was judged by the self-styled arbiters of "the Southern way of life" to be in the least "liberal." My greatest point of pride as a student journalist came when one of my editorials was denounced by a Mississippi legislator. This was seven years before James Meredith came to integrate Ole Miss, an event that provoked a bloody and destructive riot that was finally put down by Mississippi national guard troops. By then I was safely ensconced as a magazine editor in the North.

But by the time I was in college, Douglas had already graduated from the University of Missouri and returned to Mississippi where he determined to help make some changes. I didn't think of him as a hero in those days because I didn't understand what he was doing and how heroic it was. Let me put it this way: if you were a white Southerner back then and you tried to help black people, you were a hero whether you claimed the title or not.

I've always wondered why Douglas stayed and why he became so passionate about integration and civil rights. It may have had something to do with his war experiences; it may have had something to do with growing up in very meager circumstances as a child during the great depression; God knows it had nothing to do with parental influence.

He and I came from a family that didn't think enough of race as a subject that we discussed it. It never entered our consciousness even though African Americans were part of our daily lives and even though we lived and often worked shoulder to shoulder with them. Oh, we had the usual admonitions of "nice" Southern families: "Don't say nigger, say nigra or colored." And our parents referred to the black people in the county as "our nigras," using that expression in a paternal or maternal way, as in "our children," never giving a thought to how "our nigras" once meant ownership.

One time, during the Mississippi summer of 1964 when Northern blacks and whites were registering the local blacks to vote and Douglas was their visible white supporter, his mother, Aunt Cassie, trying I think to be understanding of her only son, asked him, "Douglas, what do the nigras want?"

Aunt Cassie was as sweet and abiding a person as I have ever known, a person without an interest in, or a sense of, politics despite her husband's position as a state legislator. Her question had no underlying motive, no hint of disapproval; instead, it was born of sincere curiosity and based in her understanding and acceptance of the way things had always been. In other words, it reflected what I think was the very widespread Southern characteristic of benign ignorance and apathy toward how her black neighbors were forced to live in a segregated world.

"Mama," Douglas answered, "they only want what you and I want." She shook her head and resumed cleaning her teeth with the black gum brush she always cut fresh every day, then said, "Why, Lord Lord, I thought they had all they wanted."

CHAPTER TWO

~

You're going to have to understand a little bit about our family if you want to get underneath the facts of the previous chapter and learn what Douglas was really up against.

The best place to start is with the three brothers: my father Ewart, Douglas' father Elond, and our Uncle Everson. There were two sisters, Ruvess and Valena, who, in this story, as in so many Southern stories of that generation, were minor players.

I always wondered why all the boys names started with an "E"; Mother said that it had something to do with the Bible, an explanation I was used to because it seemed that almost everything the family did had something to do with the Bible.

Our daddies' daddy was a circuit-riding preacher who caught pneumonia returning horseback from a revival meeting in 1918 and died at the age of 49. That was way before I was born so I've only heard stories about what a good man of God he was, how he would ride his horse through awful weather to comfort the sick or dying. The people loved him so much that they spent the money for a special tombstone that has a photo of him embedded in it above the words, "Too Good for Earth, God Called Him Home." You can still see the photo in the cemetery of the Pine Grove Baptist Church.

The brothers and sisters grew up on the family land, hill country with red dirt and pine trees. A few fields of bottom land and some of hillside land on which the boys spent their young days helping their preacher father scratch out a living producing a few bales of cotton and some corn to feed a few hogs and a steer or two.

Both my father and Uncle Elond had a little post-high-school education at Brown's Academy in Blue Mountain, Mississippi. Thus they were thought to be educated, and compared to most folks in that area, I guess they were. Both went on to teach school in one-room school houses, then moved on to other things. Ewart became a preacher, Elond stuck with farming and teaching, then was elected to the Mississippi legislature.

I want to be fair to Uncle Elond, but he certainly would not have influenced Douglas toward anything smacking of civil rights for blacks. In the legislature he became a great admirer of Theodore Bilbo, the senator from Mississippi who liked to tell anyone who would listen his solution to the "nigra problem." In fact, Newsman Pierre Tristam wrote that: "Bilbo ranked high and shrill among the crowded thicketry of openly racist and violence-loving American politicians."

Because he thought northern Jews were trying to stir up the colored people, Bilbo would say, and Elond agreed no doubt, "Give all the nigras a nickel and put them on a boat back to Africa. Then the Jews will follow them to get all those nickels." He didn't mean it to be funny.

People at the store laughed about that one. Even the black people laughed and poked each other and slapped their knees as if it was the funniest thing they ever heard. Laughing was the safe thing to do, I guess.

Uncle Elond and Aunt Cassie lived in a house at the top of a hill overlooking the Autry land. They had three children, Douglas and his two sisters, Laverne and Mary Jane. Although there was no real movie theater in that part of the state in 1926 when Douglas was born, Aunt Cassie apparently had enough exposure to celebrities of the day that she named her son Harold Douglas, after Harold Lloyd and Douglas Fairbanks, Jr., thus breaking the pattern of always naming the oldest son after one of the family elders.

Uncle Elond had built the house himself. It had no electricity and no plumbing right up until the mid-nineteen sixties. Water came from a cistern that collected rain from the tin roof of the house, filtering it through several layers of metal screen door screening that eventually rusted and gave the water a flavor of iron. I thought it was the best-tasting water I'd ever drunk.

He owned perhaps 180 acres of red-dirt land, with only about twenty-four tillable acres that could produce a little corn and, in a good year, a bale of cotton to the acre. Not much by any measure. He plowed the land with a mule, and while he was a church-going man, Sunday school teacher, and song leader—"choir director" being a term unheard of at the time—he was also given to angry bursts of profanity. We could hear him yelling at his mule named Preacher. His voice would echo up the hill and across the ridges: "Preacher, you son of a bitch, you better gee in there." Or, "Haw in there you son of a bitch." (Gee means right and Haw means left.)

Elond had a fierce anger and would occasionally whip the mule with a limb. He used willow switches and his belt on Douglas and the girls. I think he believed his anger was righteous because it was aimed at getting the mule or the children to do the right thing. I was scared of Uncle Elond when I was a kid, and only after entering college did I come to appreciate his intelligence and talent not to mention his sense of humor.

Whether serving in the legislature, teaching school, or leading the church choir, he worked hard at everything he did. On those hot summer days of plowing and working the fields, he'd come to the house in the middle of the day for dinner. (Supper was the evening meal.) After eating he would lie flat on the wooden front porch, take a nap, then head for the fields again, leaving a wet spot of sweat the shape of his body.

In his runs for the legislature, Uncle Elond was undefeated and mostly unopposed until after the war when a man named John Farese, who had moved to Mississippi from up North then settled in Benton County, ran against and beat Uncle Elond. "Dirty politics," Uncle Elond called it, claiming that Farese bought votes.

This event cast the Farese and Autry families as adversaries, "enemies" Uncle Elond said, for years. Oh, everyone was nice in that Southern way of condemning with kindness, but the Farese-Autry situation is what many people said was the reason Douglas got set up and sent to prison.

The irony in this for me came years later when, as a journalism student, I visited Johnny Farese in his office at the Mississippi capitol. He greeted me enthusiastically and asked if I'd like to meet the governor, then escorted me to the governor's office and introduced me, effusively describing me as an up-and-coming journalist.

I confess I was impressed by the attention and was so naïve I didn't realize that Farese had become a big name politically in the state, thus had considerable clout with the governor. Having been warned for years about him, I tried but couldn't determine any ulterior motive for his kindness, and I suspect there was none.

CHAPTER THREE

Uncle Everson, the youngest, was handsome, charming, and a ne'er-do-well and alcoholic. He also went to war at about the same time Douglas did and was crew chief on a C-47 transport in England. I remember seeing photographs he sent back, showing him smiling with his hat set at a rakish angle and crushed with what was known as a "fifty mission crush," the mark of bomber combat veterans. In other words, the fifty-mission crush on Uncle Everson was a bit misleading since he never flew on bombing missions over Germany.

After the war he returned to Benton County. His wife, Alice, died of cancer, so Everson moved elsewhere to look for work. His alcoholism generally meant he didn't hold a job for very long.

I saw him in Memphis once working as a bank guard. He looked as if he was doing well in the uniform with his badge and gun, but before long he was back in Benton County. Douglas told me Everson had lost the bank guard job when he fired his pistol into the air to prevent someone from parking illegally in the bank's parking lot.

Apparently, the bank officials had suspected him of drinking during the day but couldn't prove it because they couldn't find his bottle. After he was fired, he showed them his hiding place: in the trunk of the bank president's car.

This sounds funny and became one of the stories told at family reunions for years afterward. But Everson was not a funny man at heart. He was bitter. I can only speculate that it had something to do with the success of the older brothers and perhaps the untimely death of Aunt Alice.

It may also have had something to do with Everson having had seizures as a child. My father told me that Everson had "spells" and was given Phenobarbital. "And Ruvess and Valena babied him, and that's what ruined him," my father added.

Everson was good to me when I was a kid. He had no children of his own so he seemed to pay special attention when I was with him. He took me squirrel hunting and fishing and treated me more like a peer than a child.

I was too young to understand what he had gone through with Aunt Alice's fight with cancer. He always seemed upbeat and happy, and I didn't realize he was drinking a lot of those times.

By the time I was in college, Everson was back in Ashland, the capital of Benton County, living in a house at the edge of town and spending most of his time with his drinking buddies. He was still charming enough, I guess, to have a woman around from time to time, and he was intriguing enough, I guess—or perhaps the word is exotic—that a few married women in the town found their way to his bed.

He told Douglas that he was in hog heaven with the women, getting all the sex he could handle until one of the wives was overcome by guilt and walked down the aisle of church one Sunday and confessed her sins publicly. She named Uncle Everson as the man who had led her astray.

Everson lay low for a while, and I heard he bought a pistol in case any aggrieved husband decided to avenge his wife's damaged reputation and, of course, his own lost honor.

"My sex life slowed down a little bit after that," Everson reported later, until another wife came calling one evening. "The public confession had got her curiosity up, I reckon," he laughed, "so I satisfied it."

I came to think of Uncle Everson as a harmless and entertaining but benign presence in our family, even though the black sheep. My opinion shifted sharply in the 1960s, however, when he and his racist drinking buddies began to make Douglas' life difficult.

Chapter Four

~

My father, Ewart, the oldest brother, followed in his father's footsteps as a country preacher. At one point, he served six different churches, preaching at three of them on alternate Sundays. It was not a good way to make a living financially, so he hunted and fished and planted a large vegetable garden. He and my stepmother canned everything from squirrel and rabbit to wild blackberries. He also became a fairly successful free-lance writer of adventure stories as well as hunting and fishing articles and books.

Dad was a peace-maker, not given to arguing about religion, politics, or anything else. He would only smile at jokes or stories like the ones about Senator Bilbo, and would never pass them on. I remember one time his telling Uncle Elond that a Baptist shouldn't get too political, and that lit Elond's short fuse.

"Just because you call yourself a preacher, Ewart," Uncle Elond said, "doesn't mean you're any better Baptist than I am." Elond took pride in being a men's Sunday school teacher, and I used to think that he wanted to be the preacher after his daddy died, but my father stepped into it first, probably because he was the oldest son.

"Fact is," Uncle Elond said, "I'm a sight harder on sin than you are, to be a preacher. I don't hunt and fish with lazy, no-count drunks like you do.

Dad loved to hunt and fish and it was true that he often went with some of those old boys who used to hang around the store and the square, trying hard not to find any work to do, and always smelling of moonshine. But Dad could always justify what he did. "Elond, if you want to lead somebody to salvation, sometimes you've got to get them to trust you first so you can set an example."

This fight, like many others over the years, never lasted long. As for Uncle Everson, he pretty much stayed out of them. He probably figured it was better to avoid both of them than get caught in the middle.

I used to argue with my father that I thought most of the preachers in the South, particularly in Mississippi, were ducking the racial problem. His response was always, "Boy, I don't allow politics in my pulpit."

I think my years at the University of Mississippi effected a big change in my attitudes. I had never considered myself either racist or liberal, but as the issues of race began to be part of the public dialogue, students began to take sides. As a journalism student, I found myself among the more liberal thinkers, and as college students will do, entered into long late-night conversations about racism in the South and on the campus. I remember being shocked by the attitudes of some of the campus racists. They seemed entranced by the so-called "glorious and noble Southern cause."

It would be an overstatement to say I became radicalized, but I began to think of all that molasses-mouth stuff as utter nonsense. And yes, I became more sensitive to all the institutional things that seem to conspire to keep blacks "in their place."

My emerging attitudes didn't sit well with my family.

I tried to persuade my father that the issue was about justice and not about politics. In those years, I thought of him as cowardly and I felt he was being political in that he didn't want to offend his parishioners. I'll at least give him credit that he did not use Biblical scripture to justify racism, and years later when the Religious Right was mixing religion and politics I began to think Dad might have been right all along.

His general treatment of blacks was respectful and he acted like a peer with black preachers. But this, too, was part of the sugar coated, "be nice to everybody" Southern attitude.

Once, during the Mississippi summer of 1964 there was a rumor that a group of blacks was going to show up on a Sunday morning to integrate Dad's church. The worried deacons gathered at his home. "What are we going to do, Brother Autry, if the nigras come to church?"

Here again at Pine Grove Church was a question not unlike one its congregation faced during the Civil War. My grandfather had told the story to my father, and he had told it to me. I wonder if he had reflected on it before answering his deacons.

It was 1864. On a bright, hot Sunday as the congregation—mostly women, young boys, and old men—worshiped, a Yankee patrol galloped into the churchyard. They stopped and dismounted. A young lieutenant entered. There was a great fear, not only for life itself but for the church. Less than a mile away, a stately old house had recently been looted and put to the torch. Everyone in the congregation that morning had seen its fire, had comforted its mistress, and had tried to salvage something useable from the ashes.

But the lieutenant carried no torch and had left his pistol and saber outside.

"We saw your church from the far ridge," he said gently, "and wondered if we might worship with you. Or if you'd prefer, may we come here after you're gone?"

No one spoke, for in truth there was no spokesman. Even the minister was off to war.

"I'll go outside and let you talk about it," the lieutenant continued, "and if you decide against us, you have my word that we will leave in peace."

The decision came quickly. My great grandmother Betty Elliott, at that time a spirited young woman, led the discussion. She is said to have asked, "If we can't worship with them how are we going to live with them when this is over?" It was she who opened the door and welcomed to worship those men who were destroying her way of life.

During the Mississippi summer of 1964, Dad was very aware that there were Southerners who saw the civil rights movement as a threat to their way of life. I'm sure he had given much thought how he might answer the question about the fear of blacks coming to church, but it sounded spontaneous: "Well, we'll just give them some song books and see if they can improve the singing."

The non-answer was all the answer the deacons needed and they departed satisfied that Brother Autry could handle the situation.

CHAPTER FIVE

Chances are that Douglas would have followed in the footsteps of his father or uncles had he not gone off to war. Like most young men of his age at that time, he was eager to go even before he graduated from high school. Uncle Elond would not hear of it but was willing to sign the papers so he could join after graduation even though he was only seventeen.

Before Douglas left home, he married his school sweetheart, Elizabeth Rogers, a beautiful, dark-eyed girl who was later to be voted Miss Cunningham by Douglas's shipmates on the USS Cunningham.

In a way it's difficult to imagine the transition from the most rural of rural communities to the exotic places he would visit and the menacing duties he would face as a gunner on a destroyer.

The most excitement a boy in Benton County, Mississippi, could have in those days might be pushing an old car to its limits on the winding gravel roads. The only shooting was at rabbits or squirrels or quail. And there was not much of that because most of the game had been hunted to near extinction during the depression when people ate anything they could kill, including possum and beaver.

So think of a boy in those woods and fields, then less than a year later shooting at Kamikazes from the deck of a destroyer. The Navy had stationed a line of destroyers, referred to as the picket line, as the fleet's outer defense against Japanese attack. Douglas was a small part of that famous picket line, and he told me there were several times the sky was so full of Japanese aircraft it was like a bee hive. He didn't expect to survive, but he came out of it with only memories of near misses. Who knows what goes through the head of an 18- or 19-year old in that situation? Whatever it was, it clearly had a huge influence on Douglas' view of his world and its people.

I didn't see much of him when he was in college at the University of Missouri and only heard his stories of how the veterans on the GI Bill sort of took over the campus, made their own whiskey and beer, and generally ran roughshod over various campus protocols.

I heard of German classes held in the local pub, these stories always accompanied by little bursts of elementary German: *"Ein, zwei, drei, vier,* lift your stein and drink your beer." Douglas said that everyone got so drunk that German and English sounded the same. He claimed not to have learned much German but passed the course because the professor was a Jew who had fled Germany and who had a great appreciation for the student veterans.

Douglas was a well-known story-teller, and Elizabeth says that most of his stories of drinking and dodging his way through college were just that, "stories." She liked to say, "He wanted to make it seem that he wasn't too serious about his education." This was not an uncommon pose for Southern men who were always concerned that people might think of them as "educated fools."

Still it always struck me that Douglas did become well-educated despite all his talk about drunkenness and what in today's context seems a very benign version of debauchery.

Douglas' first job out of college was teaching school in Owensville, Missouri. Neither he nor Elizabeth was happy in Missouri. They wanted to go home to Benton County, but the only ways to make a living there were farming, selling supplies to farmers, processing the farmers' crops for market, working in one of the shirt factories in that part of the country, or being lucky enough to get a government job. And oh yes, serving in elective office.

Douglas chose the latter.

CHAPTER SIX

~

Douglas was still in College when President Truman integrated the armed forces, and he told me later that he didn't hear much about it on campus. But I remember watching a parade at the Memphis Cotton Carnival and seeing for the first time sailors from Millington Naval Air Station marching in an integrated formation. There they were, black faces in those Navy white uniforms. A lot of the Memphis people didn't like seeing that and some of the men began to yell nasty stuff at the black sailors. The sailors just looked straight ahead and kept marching.

Later, on the midway at the carnival, we saw a lot of the white sailors but no African Americans. Of course, that was because the black people had to wait for their day at the midway. No exceptions for the US Navy.

That I should have gone through my teen-age years just accepting that blacks were confined to "special days" for almost everything, the ball games, the Cotton Carnival, the Mid-South Fair, the Zoo, seems more than strange to me as I tell this story today. Just as it seems from another whole world that there were separate drinking fountains and rest rooms, not to mention schools.

And all public transportation in the South was segregated.

I recall being selected to go to the Midwest National High School Band Clinic when I was a senior. I had to ride the Greyhound Bus from Memphis to Chicago, and when we crossed the Mason-Dixon line *(an imaginary line originally surveyed between states to settle a territorial dispute, that later became the understood line between slave states and free states.)* the driver stopped the bus, turned around and said, "All right." Then most of the black people stood and moved from the back of the bus where they had been required to sit, to any empty seat they wished.

I was astonished.

A young black man sat by me.

"How you doin?" he asked.

"Fine," I answered. "How you doin?"

"Fine," he said.

Then we both slept the rest of the way to Chicago.

It was in that segregated world of the South that Douglas decided to seek elective office as County Superintendent of Education and it was in education that Douglas was to express his passion for making life better for everybody in his home county.

But first came the campaign that, as it turned out was not particularly hard fought: Douglas, local boy, combat veteran, good family, nice wife, and so on, won easily.

What he could not have imagined during those halcyon early days was that the job would turn out to be his ticket to prison.

Chapter Seven

~

When Douglas was first in the job, he loved every bit of it. He'd had some exposure to pretty good rural schools in Missouri, and he thought he could make our county schools better without too much trouble. After all, his predecessor hadn't done very much, it being wartime, and whatever Douglas did, no matter what, was bound to be better.

Whenever I'd visit, he'd be full of stories of state conventions and hanging out in the capital, of eating steaks and drinking with other county superintendents. He was making more money than he'd ever made, though still not very much by any standard outside Mississippi. He had a position in the community. He had political influence. He was, as we used to say, "in the high cotton" or "up among the high rafter bats." At least he thought he was.

I learned an expression as a second lieutenant in the Air Force that should be rendered in calligraphy, framed, and hung on the wall of every young up-and-comer, no matter the profession: "Tread Ye Ever So Softly Lest Ye Step In Shit."

Douglas did not tread softly; that is to say he did not carry out his duties carefully. He was uneducated about the basic stuff of accounting and budget management. He was generous and overly loyal to his friends. And he naively believed that people would do what they told him they would do.

Those would not seem to be unpardonable sins. But add friends who took advantage of him and political adversaries with old grudges and it becomes clear that Douglas was headed for trouble.

As Elizabeth puts it, "He was just too trusting. He hadn't learned that people use you."

At this point, I am impelled to point out that we all have our family stories, and the one about Douglas that I have lived with for sixty years is that John Farese, the man who beat Uncle Elond for a seat in the legislature, set Douglas up to be charged with a crime. But that would come later, during his first term as superintendent.

Another part of the story is that Douglas was doing too much to help the black schools which, at the time, were under the old "separate but equal" system. This work to help the black schools is a very compelling and important part of Douglas' efforts but I've discovered that, while he expressed concern about the unequal education between whites and blacks, his work with the black community comes years later.

Yet the myth of helping the black schools persisted, but how? I speculate that Douglas must have talked with too many people the way he talked with me. He was bothered by the school inequities. He told me about visiting the black school at New Salem and about being appalled by the lack of books and supplies and by the low levels of student learning. He explained to me his plan to try to get community support for more resources for the black schools.

"I'll start talking to whites about how unfair the situation is," he said with his wide and toothy smile. "I plan to talk about how unfair it is that about fifty percent of the people have to pay one hundred percent of the taxes. If I can get people to understand that, maybe I can sneak a little more money to the black schools."

He never got to work his plan, however, because racial unrest was boiling up daily all over the old Confederate states, and the atmosphere in Benton County would not have been hospitable to any attempt to shift the racial status quo.

No, this part of his story boils down to naiveté and carelessness, well-intentioned but carelessness nonetheless.

Given that, there is still strong evidence that John Farese played a role in Douglas's misfortune, but here the story gets a little baroque and begins with the relationship between Farese and Douglas' good friend Hamer McKenzie. Both men were lawyers, and after a fairly close relationship between Farese and the McKenzie family, Hamer and John had a falling out and became quite competitive.

Douglas put himself, unwittingly or not, into the middle of that by hiring Hamer as legal counsel to the county school board. I'm not sure that Farese wanted the job, but apparently he didn't want Hamer to have it. When Douglas was defeated for re-election, however, Farese was given the job.

Douglas probably also did his share of spreading the spoils, things like allotting school bus maintenance contracts, and fuel and supply-purchasing contracts to friends. He was also too casual about who could sign purchase orders, issue checks and warrants, and other such small but important tasks.

I can't imagine there ever was a Superintendent of Education who did not engage in some of this kind of petty patronage. The question is, did he get anything in return? Some said he was given a deer rifle, some said his wife got a washer and dryer (Elizabeth denies it). The generous souls in the county say he simply was too trusting and too generous for his own good and was taken advantage of by "so-called friends."

Douglas learned an old lesson the hard way: when the accusations begin you'll be criticized even for the good things you do. There is in Ashland today a school bus maintenance facility that was once the jail. When the county board of supervisors decided that the building had become too small to accommodate the demands of law enforcement in the county, they put it up for sale. Douglas saw the opportunity to turn the building into a much-needed maintenance garage.

This turned out to be bad public relations as well as of questionable legality. At the time, he was roundly criticized for wasting school district and taxpayer money to buy the building, and this became part of the growing criticism of his performance. The sticky legal issue was that, in order to put together the necessary funds, Douglas shifted money from one account to another without the formality of a budget change and without prior approval of the school board, although obviously the board of supervisors thoroughly approved the sale. This shift of funds did not pass a later audit and became part of a charge of "misappropriation of funds."

"Yet," as Elizabeth points out, "the county is still using the garage sixty years later but no one seems to remember how much condemnation Douglas had to suffer at the time."

All this was boiling up as Douglas was running for re-election. This was in the mid fifties and by then I was attending the University of Mississippi and had just turned twenty-one. I was indifferent to politics at the time, but Douglas wanted me to vote for him.

"You're a Mississippi resident, Jimmy," he said, "Come on over to Ashland and register to vote."

I felt I owed him because some of my own activities almost got him into trouble. When I'd visit, he'd loan me his car for dates. Once I took an Ashland girl to a movie and later pulled onto a road leading into the Holly Springs National Forest and parked. By today's standards, our amorous activities were relatively mild, but they were observed by a forest ranger who was on duty in the fire tower right above where I'd parked. The ranger took the license number and the word got around that Douglas was parked in a dark place with a woman obviously not his wife. Douglas not only laughed it off but told the story to his friends, embellishing it with his own considerable narrative skills. But I suspect there were those in the county who didn't believe the true story.

So I got a ride to Ashland and went to the county courthouse, a building I'd visited many times with my father, a building on whose lawn I'd watch older men play croquet and marbles, but a building whose governance role had never concerned me.

My most vivid memory of the place occurred when I accompanied my father there to take care of some sort of legal matter. I was about eleven years old.

When we started up the sidewalk toward the courthouse door, we noticed a crowd of men and boys gathered outside. One man left the group and approached my father.

"Preacher," he said, "there are a couple of niggers here who want to get married and they're looking for somebody to do it."

Dad asked why they didn't go to one of their own ministers but he didn't wait for an answer. As he walked toward the group, the men and boys made way for him. In the center was a young African American soldier in uniform. I remember the numeral "2" on his shoulder patch, indicating that he was with the Second Army in Memphis. At his side was a young woman who looked to be just a little older than I. She was smiling nervously.

Someone said, "Boy, here's a preacher. He can marry you."

Someone else said, "Make 'em jump over a broom, preacher. That's the way my granddaddy married niggers." A few men laughed, and some of the little boys giggled.

Dad ignored the man. He asked the soldier, "Won't the county clerk marry you? He can do that."

"No sir," said the soldier. "The clerk, he won't do it and I have to get back to Memphis this evening."

A man came out of the courthouse carrying a broom. He looked drunk. "Here's a broom. Make 'em jump a broom." My father frowned and a couple of the men intercepted the drunk and turned him back into the courthouse.

Dad took over the scene the way I'd seen him do many times. "Everybody stand back and give these folks some room." Then he directed the solder and his fiancé to stand side by side facing him, and he told me to stand back with the other boys.

"We are gathered here," he began, and one of the men laughed and some of the boys giggled. Dad stopped and looked at the man, then at the boys. He didn't say anything; he didn't have to. Everyone fell silent.

As Dad performed the service, it seemed to me that the men and boys became very serious. No one spoke, no one laughed or even smiled. When one of the boys giggled, his father thumped him on the back of the head.

"I now pronounce you man and wife. You may salute the bride."

The soldier looked confused. "You may kiss her," Dad said, but the couple shook their heads. This set off shouts from the group.

"Kiss her, boy, let's see you kiss her." The little boys giggled again.

"How much do I owe you, preacher?" the soldier asked.

"You don't owe me anything.'

"No, sir," said the soldier, "I appreciate it but I want to pay you."

"A dollar'll do," said Dad.

The soldier paid, then he and his bride walked out to an old pickup truck, got in, and drove away.

The crowd began to disperse. Some of the men shook their heads. Others laughed.

Now, ten years later, I was walking across that same ground and thinking again of that episode, as I did every time I visited the courthouse, and also thinking that not much had changed in those ten years.

I went in to register with the county clerk, my Cousin Lawson Mathis. He pulled out a worn stack of papers and said, "Here, Jimmy, read this and tell me what it means." He was holding a section of the Constitution.

I knew this was one of the ways that white people kept black people from voting. I didn't like it, and being a smart aleck college student at the time, I said, "Cousin Lawson, the US Supreme Court has been trying to interpret this constitution for a long time. How do you expect me to do it?"

Cousin Lawson looked at me with irritation, then glanced around and said, "That's good enough. You're registered."

The first time I ever voted was for my cousin Douglas to be re-elected Superintendent of Education.

He was defeated, but it was probably just as well because within a few months Douglas was charged with embezzlement and brought to trial.

Chapter Eight

A state audit of the Benton County school district for the years 1953 and 1954 revealed, or seemed to reveal, that about $78,000 dollars was missing. The audit indicated that some of the funds were allegedly embezzled while others were misappropriated.

In separate legal actions, Douglas was charged in a criminal case of embezzlement and also was one of the defendants, along with the members of the county board of education, in a civil suit brought by the State of Mississippi for recovery of funds. Included in the funds to be recovered was the cost of the jail that Douglas purchased and converted into the school bus maintenance garage, using funds not appropriated for that purpose. *(It's the same garage still used by the county today.)*

In the latter case, the chancery court rendered judgment in favor of the state in the amount of $13,879.

In trying to determine the final disposition of the case, I was told by Elizabeth that the state settled with the school board's bonding company for only the cost of the trial, the implication being that the big money was not missing but was misspent, a civil and not a criminal matter.

It was the embezzlement trial in August of 1956, however, that got all the attention.

August is very likely the most unpleasant time to be in Mississippi. In those days, it was popular for city newspapers in the South to publish photos of eggs frying on the sidewalks while warning people to stay out of the sun and to not over-exert themselves. I remember the presence of salt tablet dispensers in retail businesses and office buildings, as a protection against heat exhaustion.

The temperatures are bad enough but the humidity makes you feel as if you're breathing steam. It is not a time for coat and tie, but the trial brought coat-and-tied news reporters streaming into Ashland from newspapers in Memphis, Jackson, and Tupelo, among other places.

The trial was considered big news in Ashland and north Mississippi, and reporters searching for something to write began interviewing anyone who'd talk about Douglas or the trial or both. One newspaper reported that, "Each day of the trial found the tiny Ashland square filled with cars from as many as eight Mississippi counties and several from out of state."

Early in 1956, Elizabeth and Douglas, again out of a job after having lost the election, had rented a building on the square and opened the City Café. It was a typical small town café. Up front there was a counter on one side of a corridor type room, and booths on the other side. The back room, the "banquet room," was a large square with tables and chairs to sit about sixty. On grainy wood paneling hung large framed paintings of Black Angus cattle and photographs of champion hunting dogs. There was no other attempt at atmosphere because in a town like Ashland, a restaurant lived or died on the quality of its food. Elizabeth and her helpers served good southern fare: breakfast, plate lunches, and sandwiches, all of it on café dishes. This was before Styrofoam.

One newspaper noted the irony that, "The café did a landslide business during the Autry trial. Mrs. Autry, attractive brunette, served banana cream pie to customers while her husband was on trial. The juke box blared rock and roll. Autry sat in a back booth laughing and his wife did the same in a front booth just before the judge passed sentence."

The *Tupelo Daily Journal* featured the trial on the front page from the day jury selection began on August 21.

It's not that this was a slow news time. Nationally, the Republican Convention was going strong in San Francisco, and Eisenhower had arrived there the night before.

Meanwhile in Mississippi, Mississippians for States Rights were threatening to oppose the national Democratic Party in order to throw the presidential election into the House of Representatives, declaring that "it would be impossible to find two men more obnoxious to our way of life than Adlai Stevenson and Estes Kefauver." In another story, Governor J. P. Coleman was quoted as supporting Stevenson.

Across the August 22nd front page, Ex-President Hoover was warning against "all-powerful government," while in another story Harold Stassen was trying to lead a "dump Nixon" movement on the floor of the GOP convention.

But there, in the middle of the page was "Douglas Autry Jury is Chosen." The day before, the jury had been reported as "snarled." The trial was speedy indeed because on the 23rd, the Journal bannered a four-column headline: "Impassive Autry Found Guilty of Embezzlement."

Although the family suspected John Farese of having his hand somehow in Douglas' predicament, I have no proof, not that it matters much these years later.

Elizabeth told me about one meeting that, if her memory is accurate, would prove that Farese was at the least a very interested observer. Elizabeth put it more bluntly: "Johnny was out to get Hamer, and he tried to use Douglas to do it."

She described the meeting as having taken place in an office at the bank. Her memory of the timing is vague; it was either right before the trial began or right after. Attending were Elizabeth's father Mr. Whit Rogers, John Farese, my cousin the banker Booth Grisham, and Douglas. I suspect that Mr. Rogers had been convinced that the meeting could help his son-in-law and thus, his daughter and granddaughter.

According to Mr. Rogers, Farese said to Douglas, "If you will agree to testify against Hamer McKenzie about his role in this, you won't even have to go back to the courtroom."

Douglas's response: "Go to hell."

You might wonder how Farese could even make such an offer, but in a state where the judges are elected and depend, as all politicians do, on influence and campaign contributions, and where county attorneys are frequently cozy with the local political establishment, it's not difficult to believe that a well-known lawyer and politician might be able to influence the proceedings of an ongoing trial. Even today, situations like these make headlines in Mississippi.

But Douglas' "Go to Hell" defense of his friend Hamer meant that there was no intervention on his behalf. After reading newspaper stories and appellate court records, I'm convinced that, while Douglas participated in something that was judged to be embezzlement, there was more to it than was ever publicly revealed.

It even struck me that the prosecuting attorney's summary, though it was clearly in the overwrought mode of normal Mississippi courtroom theatrics, still excessively dramatized the amount of the embezzlement.

The District Attorney told the jury that ". . .your money flowed down Corruption Creek that day; that's what happened."

Fully wound up, he shouted, this ". . .is more money than some Benton County Farmers will clear off a crop this year." Then he asserted that this money "would buy hot lunches for 50 school kids. . .would buy 500 school books. . .would furnish one schoolroom." He effectively made it look as if Douglas, whose life was devoted to educating the children of Benton County, had instead taken food and books away from them. No one questioned the accuracy of those particular claims.

According to the *Tupelo Daily Journal*, the trial "upset all popular and court predictions as to the outcome. The

Autry jury also became the first Benton County jury in 25 years to be locked up for the night."

I don't know all the details, and most of the participants in the indictment, trial, and conviction are dead or very elderly. I do know the result, however, and it smells awfully fishy.

Douglas was sentenced to seven years in the infamous Mississippi Prison, Parchman Farm, for embezzling $630.

Chapter Nine

~

The paradox of small towns, wherever in America they are, is that the people are as generous and as supportive as they are vindictive and unforgiving. Often the same people and at the same time. I call it courteous animosity. And they seem quick to condemn a whole family for the transgressions of one of its members. Thus, Elizabeth had a hard time.

With Douglas in prison, Elizabeth was left to run the business and try to keep some money coming in. But it wasn't easy. It should go without saying that the citizens of Ashland all considered themselves to be good Christians, and what I know about those good small-town Christians in the South is that many of them take great comfort in the sins of others.

Elizabeth recalls one day, after Douglas was shipped off to Parchman Farm, a man came into the café and told her that she should be ashamed to show her face in

Ashland and that she should move away. As if somehow she was as culpable as her husband was judged to be.

As for Douglas, he spent his prison days at menial tasks such as working with leather to make wallets and purses and so on. I still have a wallet he made and sent me from Parchman Farm.

One of the most admirable aspects of Douglas' personality was his ability to be comfortable with anyone and to make anyone feel comfortable. He was a disarmingly bright person. He dressed like a farmer and talked with the drawl and the many colloquialisms, some raucous and crude, of a Benton County country boy, but could make his points like the college graduate he was. He was a story-teller and could find the humor in most situations. He also had an uncanny ability to bring out the best in people, whether friends or adversaries.

I suspect these traits served him well in prison. I know he was proud of the nickname the other prisoners gave him. In Mississippi, as in many other states, the governor appoints "Colonels" in the state "militia" or reserves. This is purely an honorary title, without authority, duties, or compensation, given to recognize political allies. *(I'm an Iowa Colonel appointed by the governor. Big deal.)*

Governor J. P. Coleman had appointed Douglas a colonel early in his term, so when this became known among his fellow prisoners they began to call him Colonel. He told me that meant as much to him as when the governor appointed him.

I never heard him complain about prison, or even talk about it much, but Elizabeth visited him every week, driving the 130 miles to the prison from their home in Ashland, and she said he hated the place and the life there. Because of the frequent visits, they didn't exchange one letter during his term. After he was released, he refused to talk to anyone, including me, about the experience.

Douglas served only 18 months before his sentence was commuted and he left Parchman Farm never to return. He was also legally prohibited from "any political activity or public controversy of any kind whatsoever." A few years later, Governor Ross Barnett granted him a full and complete pardon which restored his "franchise and citizenship rights."

CHAPTER TEN

~

Douglas told me that when he first was released he was inclined to just get out of Benton County, feeling that he would not be able to re-enter the community and that probably no one would employ him. But he was concerned about his parents, both of whom suffered with arthritis, so he decided to stay and when his father-in-law offered him a job on his farm, Douglas was happy to get it.

He had left his father's farm for the Navy, and had gone to college so he wouldn't have to return to farming. Now here he was again, but he engaged it with energy and with appreciation that he was at least free and working at something that was necessary and that made a difference. It sure beat the Hell out of making leather wallets. He spent six years farming and running the café with Elizabeth.

When I talk to people in the county these days, those who remember seem to agree that Douglas was "railroaded," or in the words of Willie Ruth Daugherty, now director of the Benton County Community Action Program, "Douglas took the rap for others." I'm sure there are those who disagree, but if so I couldn't find them after all these years, and every African American I talked with agreed. It seemed a common assumption in the black community.

When he returned to the county, though, it took a lot of courage for Douglas to do the ordinary community things that were second nature to everyone else. Some people were openly hostile, others just quietly ignored him, passing him on the street without speaking.

I thought Douglas must have been born to be a maitre d', a down-home one at the very least. It always seemed to me that Elizabeth and her few helpers did the cooking and serving work in the café, while Douglas greeted the customers.

"I found out who my friends really were," he said later. And as the years passed, he made new friends, many of whom were black. He didn't know it at the time, but he was about to get his chance to influence race relations in a way he'd thought about when he was superintendent —but this time it wasn't through the schools.

As Bob Dylan was to sing a few years later, "the times they are a-changin'." Douglas' post-prison years were those in which John F. Kennedy was elected president and was assassinated. They were years in which the Vietnam War was begun and expanded. They were years of protest and riot.

In the midst of all that, they were also years of positive change and crucial legislation. Kennedy put in place some initiatives that came to fruition under Johnson. One of them was the Economic Opportunity Act of 1964 that combined new programs with existing programs under a different approach called Community Action Programs (CAP), including such things as Head Start and the Neighborhood Youth Corps (NYC).

Douglas could not have imagined that what was going on in Washington would change his life forever, would give him the opportunity to do what he had wanted to do since he came home from the Navy: help the poor people of Benton County and Mississippi, particularly African Americans.

Elizabeth says, "It caused Douglas physical pain to see people in poverty. He literally couldn't stand it, and he always wanted to do something about it. And it didn't make any difference whether the people were black or white. He wanted to help them."

The Community Action Program was to give him that opportunity. As further evidence of Douglas' comment that Faulkner wasn't making up anything about the baroque relationships in Mississippi towns and families, but was just writing it down, it was John Farese's nephew Tony Farese who was the catalyst of Douglas' opportunity. Tony came to Douglas one day in 1964 and asked if he wanted a job.

Considering the feud, imagined or otherwise, between our family and the Fareses, I asked Elizabeth why Tony Farese would have helped Douglas. Her answer was typically Southern and rendered with a matter-of-factness that, it seemed to me, foreclosed any further questions: "Tony was the best of the Fareses."

Douglas thus became Director of the Neighborhood Youth Corps in Benton and part of another county. Later he was to be made acting director for the nine-county region.

Chapter Eleven

The Community Action Programs in Benton County were housed in a building originally intended as a county clinic, but the one and only doctor in town had his own office and refused to practice in the clinic. Thus it was only minimally used for health services.

The government had built it with the best intentions but apparently with no plan for staffing. Most people thought it a waste, and it became a symbol of all the "dumb things the government does with our money." (Of course at the time, federal dollars coming into Mississippi far outweighed, by perhaps 100 to one, the tax dollars going out of the state.)

Thus the mostly empty clinic became the perfect place for the CAP, and it was there that Douglas as head of the Neighborhood Youth Corps became a presence in the community again.

I had returned from the Air Force by then and was working as a magazine editor in Des Moines, Iowa, or as the Benton county folks put it, "up north." I returned from time to time for hunting and fishing trips and to visit family.

I visited Douglas' NYC office for the first time during one of those trips. He introduced me to his assistant, Walter Webber, a black man. Walter asked me if I was planning to hunt birds or rabbits. I said, "Birds," and he mentioned a few good hunting places in the northern part of the county.

It seemed a normal conversation for a couple of southern men to have, even for a black and white to have, but what impressed me was the straightforwardness of it. I called him Walter. He called me Jimmy, not Mr. Jimmy. I extended my hand when we met; he shook it assertively rather than diffidently. This may seem small stuff these days but in 1965 this was a meaningful signal of an assumption of equality by both of us, a small harbinger of the change that was coming.

Then Douglas looked at his watch and said, "Let's go visit Head Start." We went down the hall to a waiting area. On one side of the hall sat white women; on the other side, black. Douglas greeted the women, "It's about that time." They nodded and smiled, and Douglas continued to engage them, addressing both black and white as "Mrs. _____."

Douglas was adamant about his balanced courtesy toward both groups of women. The white women called him "Douglas," but the black women in the manner of Southern African Americans at that time called him, "Mr. Douglas," despite his telling them to call him Douglas.

"This is a matter of dignity," he once explained to me. "These folks have been called by their first names or by some damned patronizing thing like 'Uncle' or 'Aunt' all their adult lives. Before that, they were called 'girl' or 'boy.' Did you know that most of the newspapers in the South refuse to refer to black people as Mr. or Mrs.?"

I did know that because I had worked as a copy boy at *The Commercial Appeal* in Memphis and remembered seeing a delegation of well-dressed African American men calling on the editor. I learned they were simply trying to get the policy changed so black people would be referred to as Mr. or Mrs. or Miss.

Douglas checked his watch again. "Watch this," he said under his breath to me, continuing to smile at the women. A door opened with the sound of children laughing and chattering. They came through the door, some hand in hand, little black and white kids together. Only their mothers were segregated.

As we headed back to his office, Douglas said, "A lot of people in this county would go crazy if they could see those kids together. They wash their hands, brush their teeth, go to the bathroom together. And their mothers are learning a lot, but I doubt that they go home and brag about what they see."

I confess I was amazed myself. Again, this doesn't seem very radical today, but then, in the 36th poorest county in the US, Head Start was about as radical an experiment as I could imagine. It was radical in its assumption that blacks and whites sharing bathroom facilities was the norm; it was radical in the fact that black and white kids would be overtly affectionate toward one another; and it was radical in what it taught the mothers about their shared experiences and similarities.

And this was well before the schools in Benton County were integrated.

Once, when I asked Douglas to explain about the Neighborhood Youth Corps and what specifically he did, he laughed. "Let's go to the café," he said, "and I'll explain it to you." So we drove several blocks to the café he and Elizabeth still owned, across the street from the courthouse where his county superintendent's office had been. We ordered coffee and Douglas lit one of the little cigars that he smoked constantly and that contributed to his death years later.

"What I do," he said, "is I try to get jobs for high school drop-outs then if possible cycle them back into school. If not that, at least it keeps them doing something worthwhile and not hanging around with nothing to do but get into trouble."

"Who gives them the jobs?"

"Well that's part of the problem. I persuade local businesses to do it, and of course the government funds the salaries so it doesn't cost the business guys anything. But it's harder than you think. We also have classes to provide some education these kids never got, and we do job training as well as teach such stuff as personal hygiene. A lot of these kids never take baths, have never brushed their teeth, and we've had girls who didn't even understand their menstrual periods or what to do about that. And I'm talking about the poor whites as well as the blacks."

He paused and drew on the cigar and greeted people entering the café. Our conversation was to be interrupted every time anyone entered or departed. Douglas, taking the role of proprietor, smiled and gave the usual southern hello or goodbye, something like, "Come on in here and get comfortable" or "Come on in here out of the weather" or "Y'all better stay a while longer" or "Come back and see us."

Growing up in the South, I rarely heard anyone say hello or goodbye. There was always this little social ritual. At Abel's store, where for many decades my family had done business, my father never left the premises without saying, "Go with us!" Then someone would answer, "No, preacher, you better go with us." Or they might promise to fix a little dinner. "We'll find something around the house to make the gravy smell good." Of course, no one ever accepted an invitation.

As an impatient college student, I remember thinking what a bunch of nonsense this was. Later I learned a little something about the importance of lubricating the gears of social concourse (as I liked to put it).

I asked Douglas what made it so hard to place the kids in jobs.

"Think about it, Jimmy," he said. "Who are most of the drop-outs?"

"Poor kids?"

"And who's poor around here? Both white and black kids. I have a hell of a time getting jobs for the black kids, government money or no government money, and most of the good middle-class folks here still use the term 'poor white trash.'"

That's the only explanation of the job I ever heard.

I talked about the program with Walter Webber in 2009. He greeted me by saying, "I've fooled around and got to be an old man since I saw you last." He was 88 years old.

Walter explained that when the program began, there were no books and no established curriculum for the classes.

"Douglas and I used to go to meetings in Corinth over in Tippah County. They had an old school over there so we asked them could we have those old books? They said, 'Take all you want.' So we loaded up those old books and used them to start our classes. Some of the kids couldn't even read."

I asked how they developed the curriculum. 'Well," Walter said, "we didn't fool too much with a formal curriculum. Both Douglas and I been school teachers so we just took the books we had and wrote a curriculum to match the books."

"So you just sort of made it up as you went along?" I asked.

"That's right. We had about a hundred and fifty kids and some of them did all right. We had something called the California test. We'd give the kids that test, and the ones that passed, we'd take and enroll in Northeast Mississippi Junior College."

He paused, then said, "We had some hard days. Finally we got good books and good materials."

I learned that Douglas, when he was not traveling to Corinth and other communities for which he had responsibility, would spend some time most days at the café. From there he could walk the square, calling on merchants and other businesspeople, selling his youth corps "clients" as good employees.

The mid-sixties were an unsettled time in Mississippi. James Meredith had integrated the university in 1962, an episode that seemed to draw every racist charlatan and fool in the country to Oxford, Mississippi. The ensuing riot and its aftermath dominated the news for weeks.

It was only two years later that the CAP was created, so Douglas faced a lot of residual anger about "forced integration." Exacerbating that anger, from Douglas' point of view, was the influx of people responding to the call to go to Mississippi and register black voters. This was the infamous "Mississippi summer of 1964."

Douglas was right, of course. It was a terrible time in Mississippi. Visiting civil rights protesters and workers, both black and white, were being harassed, often beaten, and even murdered. I remember being concerned about visiting the state because of the Iowa license plates on my car. Any "northern" car might be judged to be carrying "Yankee trouble-makers."

Many of the white and black northerners who came South didn't just come for that infamous summer. Some of them stayed on, and others came throughout the next year or two. The ones who came to Benton County congregated at the clinic, as the offices were still known locally, which meant that when Douglas started the Neighborhood Youth Corps, his office became a center of activity. It also became known as a friendly and hospitable place, despite Douglas' concerns that the whole Mississippi summer effort and its aftermath had spawned violence in the state.

But with all that, there was very little evidence of violence in Benton County. Still, Douglas' support of black people, both through the NYC and his personal friendliness to the visitors, did not make him popular with many of the county's white people.

He didn't care. I think he probably felt that if the local people hadn't supported him through his trial and conviction and his return from prison, it didn't matter whether they supported him now or not.

His greater concern was that his African American staff were often treated rudely or verbally abused. Walter Webber told me, "You could always count on Douglas to go to bat for you." He explained that whenever there was an incident, even a minor one, Douglas would find the abuser and, as Walter put it, "in a nice friendly way confront him and get him to promise not to do it again." He laughed, "Then he'd thank the person for cooperating."

I can only describe the fear of integration as irrational. Little things sent shock waves. Once in the café, Douglas was at his customary place at the counter during a busy lunch period when several young northerners, both black and white, entered.

Everything in the café stopped. People looked at Douglas. He said, "Y'all come on in," then to Elizabeth, "Lib, see if you can find these folks a place to sit."

A few white people got up and left, most stayed. Douglas poured the visitors coffee and made some small talk. I'm sure this incident was known throughout the entire county by sundown.

Of course, about 50% of the county was African American, which meant that Douglas' popularity in the black community was becoming even stronger with every report of these incidents.

On the other hand, while Douglas supported the goals of equal rights and voter registration, he was not altogether supportive of the northern visitors.

"Hell, we've got CoFo, we've got CORE and SNICK and the NAACP and a bunch of others you never heard of," he told me. "It has become a power struggle and if you think it's confusing to us, think of those black folks out in the county trying to figure out which ones to support."

Elizabeth interrupted, "But they've been better organized lately."

"You're right," Douglas responded, "I'll give them that. Of course if they don't get together they'll never help anybody. They've often been their own worst enemies."

Then he told the story of the black school principal. "The segregationists love this story," he said, "because it makes all too good a point for them."

The story goes that one of the black school principals refused to let some of the "Mississippi Project" workers enter his classes. "These young people must use their school time to study," he had explained.

Douglas said he thought the principal did the right thing but, he continued, "Certain civil rights groups pressured officials until the 'Uncle Tom' principal was dismissed. Then later, the principal won a several thousand dollar court judgment against the groups.

"When blacks go against blacks like that, it's very confusing for many of our black citizens and it really hurts the cause." He paused, "But like Libby said, it's getting better and it will get better.

"There's only one really bad result I can see that's come out of all this civil rights activity." I remember how truly sad he looked when he said, "The Klan."

DOUGLAS AUTRY
1952-1956
1976-1988

Douglas Autry served as Benton County Superintendent of Education for one term in the fifties and then three terms leading up to his retirement in 1988.

Elond Autry, Douglas' father who was a farmer, school teacher, song leader, and legislator. After many years as a segregationist he was influenced by Douglas and became President of the county school board and worked to help oversee the racial integration of the schools.

Douglas as head of the Neighborhood Youth Corps in the seventies.

The author, left, and Everson Autry who headed the KKK in the county and harassed Douglas, his nephew.

The original Autry siblings, circa 1976. Seated left to right: Ewart, Elond (Douglas' father), and Everson. Standing: Valena, left, and Ruvess.

The infamous Mississippi prison Parchman Farm (top and bottom) where Douglas was incarcerated for eighteen months.

Benton County Courthouse, in which Douglas was tried and convicted.

Ashland high school, which was whites only until integration.

New Salem school and shop. African Americans only.

A crowded classroom at New Salem school.

Chapter Twelve

~

I grew up hearing about the Ku Klux Klan but never saw any except in photographs of them in their sheets and hoods. They simply had no presence in the Benton County of my childhood and youth.

In fact, my father used to brag about the relationship between blacks and whites and often told stories of how he would go fishing with black men, how blacks and whites would work together to help rebuild someone's house that had burned. He particularly liked to tell about how the white and black Abel's Store community rallied to rebuild the home of an elderly black woman. This helping-others-in-hard-times kind of integration seemed a point of pride with him.

But that was a far cry from the kind of integration that black leaders desired. The schools were still segregated in the mid-sixties. There were still separate water fountains and rest rooms for blacks and whites. Blacks still sat in the back of the bus. In some towns, blacks still stepped off the sidewalk to let whites pass. The rest of it—the hunting and fishing together, the occasional communal helping of someone in need, the social greetings at the store—was just the veneer covering the racial reality of southern life.

And black people wanted change. It was boiling up everywhere, and Benton County, which had long languished in relative isolation from the larger world, was feeling the pressure.

The local newspaper was *The Southern Advocate* whose motto was "We Favor Continuous Progress," an uncontroversial slogan if there ever was one, did not, as an unwritten policy, publish news of people in the black community. So in 1964, a group of local black citizens began to publish a mimeographed paper called *Benton County Freedom Train*. It's motto was "One Man-One Vote."

Volume one, number three, of the *Benton County Freedom Train* features a cover drawing of the planet earth with five cartoon characters, three black and two white, holding hands atop the globe. There are articles on "Why Non-Violence," along with admonitions to vote and to "know your rights." In one letter to the editor, the writer asserts that, "The whites are not free either. The way they treat the Negroes. . . .enslaves everyone."

The tone sharpened a bit by Volume two, the cover of which features a drawing of freedom marchers bearing signs, "Montgomery," "Selma," "Holly Springs," and "Greenwood." In the foreground are two black men, one saying to the other, "They want to know where to march next. How about Ashland? (the capital of Benton County)"

So Douglas was operating in an increasingly tense environment, and he was correct in saying that there were a lot of white people who would have gone crazy had they seen the very integrated Head Start program.

The integration in his own Neighborhood Youth Corps program was far more challenging than Head Start, principally because the kids were older and had already developed their racist attitudes. To put it bluntly, the white kids wouldn't go to classes with the blacks.

Walter Webber remembers his frustration in trying to persuade the whites to come to class. "I told them that it was a requirement of the program that they had to have the class training. I told them, now that they dropped out of school, this was their education. It didn't make a difference to them. They said the schools weren't integrated and that the NYC should have separate classes for the races."

So Walter talked with Douglas. The youth received a salary funded by the federal government and administered by the NYC for their participation in the program, both as an employee of one of the local businesses and as a student in the classes.

"Well," Douglas told Walter, "I've heard that money talks. We'll see how loud it talks. We won't pass out their checks until after the last class of the week. They'll have to show up for all of them and sit through all of them or they won't get a check."

"It worked," Walter says. "I think we had the first integrated classroom in Benton County. And man, they didn't like it and griped about it and got some of the adults to talk to us and so on. But we told them rules are rules." He pauses and smiles, "The kids got used to it and after a while it didn't seem to make a difference to them anymore."

As Willie Ruth Daugherty puts it, "Douglas Autry was definitely ahead of his time in the South."

But the whole subject of integration made a difference to some of the adults in Benton County. At the time one of the great debates in the state was between those who would rather close the schools than integrate them and those who wanted to keep the schools open and face up to the integration mandate. The legislature had threatened to close the schools while groups like the Mississippi Economic Council were supporting public education all the way.

This was also the period during which the infamous White Citizens Councils were becoming a strong presence in the state. They had begun in 1954 as a response to the famous Brown v. Board of Education ruling by the Supreme Court.

They were not the Ku Klux Klan, still they used economic and social pressure to intimidate citizens into their point of view. Unlike the Klan, the WCC met openly and was seen by many as being "reputable"; in most communities there was little or no stigma associated with being a member of the WCC. In fact, the WCC was even referred to during the civil rights era as "an uptown Klan," "a white collar Klan," "a button-down Klan," and "a country club Klan." The rationale for these nicknames was that it appeared that sheets and hoods had been discarded and replaced by suits and ties.

These groups were also the source of funds and organizing efforts to establish "White Academies" as a segregated private school alternative to public schools. The problem was, and would continue to be, the tuition cost more than many families could afford.

So to those in Benton County who were committed to keeping the schools segregated, the whole idea of a high-school level integrated classrooms was anathema. Douglas began to get threatening notes and phone calls. He ignored them.

When I asked Douglas about the Klan, he said, "Well, I'm not sure it's the organized Klan with all its silly rituals and so on, but they call themselves the Klan. It's mainly a bunch of no-count do-nothings who hang around the square."

The Klan leader and his good old boys had set up a café across the square to compete with Douglas and Elizabeth's. "They plan to get the racist customers," Douglas said.

One night, the local Klan burned a cross in his front yard. Douglas ignored even this incident, but on another evening, someone tried to force Douglas' wife Elizabeth off the road between her house and town. Then soon after, the head of the Klan blocked the sidewalk in front of Douglas' 13-year-old daughter Becky as she was walking to a beauty parlor on the other side of the square from her parents' café. He called her a nigger lover and told her she should be ashamed of what her daddy was doing.

This was too much for Douglas. He marched across the square to the café, went in, and as soon as the head Klansman saw him, he said, "Douglas, I didn't know anything about the thing with Elizabeth. And I don't know who did it."

"Well, you know who scared Becky and called her a nigger lover. It was you, and by God, Chick, if you pull any of this shit again with my family I'm going to come over here and whip your fat ass."

Chick, of course, was the nickname of our Uncle Everson, who now headed the KKK in Benton County and who was to continue his harassment of Douglas for years to come.

Chapter Thirteen

As I've said, Uncle Everson was good to me as a kid and always seemed upbeat and fun-loving whereas most of the family, good Southern Baptists all, seemed to think that life was about hard work and strong faith and not much time for foolishness. Foolishness was definitely part of Everson's life, and this is probably what drew both Douglas and me to him. He was simply fun to be with, that is, until his drinking dragged him down.

My first wife always thought that Uncle Everson was the most charming man in the family, possibly including me, and he certainly seemed to have an attraction for women. Some of the men around town used to joke about just what physical characteristics made him so successful with his parade of "lady friends," a success that continued even after he became greatly overweight.

There was a standard description in our family for someone who was overweight, or was becoming that way: "Lord, Lord, he's (or she's) getting big as Uncle Bob." The story was that my Great-Uncle Bob got so heavy the boys in the family had to carry him from his chair to the dinner table.

Naturally then, I once said to Douglas that I believe Uncle Everson was getting big as Uncle Bob. Douglas replied, "No, bigger than Uncle Bob."

And the older Everson grew, the more obese he became. He finally got so fat that once when he sneezed he cracked a rib. Even he laughed about it. "Boys," he said to us, "looks like I'm gonna have to give up sneezing."

I think it was his general good humor and lighthearted approach to life that caused me to be so surprised by the hostility he developed toward black people. Everson got to the point he seemed to detest even looking at African Americans. Douglas and I couldn't understand it. Everson's experiences of hunting and fishing with black people and generally being around them was the same as any of our experiences in those days.

But his personality became darker during the unrest of the 1960s and he seemed always mad about something and most of the time it was about black people. When he heard the story about Bilbo and his plan for the Jews and Negroes, Everson acted as if he thought it was more than a joke, that it would be a good thing to give the black folks a nickel apiece and put them on the boat to Africa so the Jews would follow them to get the nickel.

In 1967 my son Rick was stricken with epilepsy. The neurologists indicated that if there was any epilepsy in our family it might indicate that Rick would grow out of his seizures. So I questioned everyone in the family about the possibility of seizures. Finally, my father recalled that "Everson had spells when he was little."

No one else in the family claimed to remember anything about it, so with only Dad's comment to go on, I decided to visit Uncle Everson and ask him directly. Of course this meant going to his "café" on the square.

On the door was a sign, "Members Only." It was summer and even though Benton was a "dry" county, I could smell the faint odor of whiskey mixed with the body odor of Everson's no-count buddies. I peered through the screen and Everson recognized me.

"Is that you, Jimmy?" he called. "Come on in here."

I entered.

"It says 'members only,' Uncle Everson," I said, walking over to where he sat.

"Let me see your hand," he said.

He took it, opened it and looked at the palm, and laughed.

"That's white enough. You're a member." His buddies laughed.

I explained about the epilepsy and told him it would be important to me and Rick if he could remember something about his spells. He looked a little embarrassed, and I was reminded again how epilepsy was still stigmatized at that time, particularly in rural areas. Many conservative Christians consider (or considered) epilepsy to be "possession by demons." In fact, there were pharmacies that sold the seizure medications in packages that camouflaged the contents.

He told me to pull a chair close, then, glancing furtively at his friends, told me how he really didn't remember much about the spells but that he had to take "little white pills" every day.

"Phenobarbital?" I asked.

"I think that was it," he said, "and I took them until I went into the army." He also told me he never had a spell after he stopped taking them. (This was a good sign for my son, and indeed Rick stopped having seizures and was able to discontinue his anticonvulsant drugs when he was twenty-three years old.)

I thanked Everson profusely and started to leave.

"Stay with me and talk a while," he said.

So I asked him the standard southern question: "What you been up to lately?"

"I guess Douglas has told you," he said.

"Yes, he said you and your friends were giving him a hard time."

"Well, shit," Everson said, "He's helping the niggers ruin this county."

"I don't agree with you, Everson," I said. "We're way overdue for change down here, and the South isn't going to make any real progress until the race problem gets solved."

"Seems like you moved up North and became one of them fuzzy-headed liberals, Jimmy."

"No, by Mississippi standards, I was a fuzzy-headed liberal before I moved up North, Uncle Everson. And frankly I confess I'm glad I'm not down here trying to solve these problems like Douglas is."

"Well my way of solving it is different from Douglas.'"

"What's got you so riled up?" I asked. "Hell, you and I have been around black people all our lives."

"Have you seen those little white Yankee girls down here with those big black bucks?" He paused. "I saw that when I was stationed in England during the war. That's what they want, white women."

I'd heard this junk almost all my life, even in college, and I knew this conversation would not go anywhere productive, so I asked him what else was bothering him.

"Jobs," he said loudly so his friends could hear him. They nodded vigorously. "They want to take the good jobs away from white people."

I looked around at the group. If I had thrown a rock at them I would not have hit one who had seriously looked for a job in years. How can I put this? Perhaps in the language of those self-same good ole boys: they were as sorry a looking bunch of drag-ass do-nothings as I had ever seen. It was time for me to leave.

"Come back and see me when you can stay a while," Everson called in his friendly-as-ever Southern style of saying goodbye.

CHAPTER FOURTEEN

Douglas was a loving son who respected Uncle Elond's service as a legislator, teacher, choir director, and church man, and he appreciated Aunt Cassie's gentle way of doing all those things a farm wife and mother must do. Life was not easy for either of them.

Uncle Elond plowed his mule, raised milk cows and hogs, and Aunt Cassie kept house, cooked, sewed, and churned butter from the fresh milk. The children helped in the garden, fed the livestock, and milked the cows.

On washday, Douglas or his father would hitch the mule to a sled and take laundry supplies down the hill and through the woods to Autry creek. There, on a level area, the family kept two large black wash pots turned upside down. Douglas would turn over the pots, carry water from the creek to fill them, and build a fire. One pot was for washing, the other for rinsing.

While the laundry was being done, Uncle Elond would take the mule to plow or do other heavy chores, then return with the mule and sled to pull the finished laundry back up the hill to be hung in the sun on clothes lines to dry. Sometimes sheets and bedding would be draped on shrubs and small trees.

All this can sound idyllic to those who haven't experienced the relentless demands of country life and livestock 365 days a year and in all kinds of weather. It was hard as Hell and often perilous.

The milk cows were allowed to graze through the woods and fields, so every day, one of the children had to go "get up the cows," which meant find them and drive them back up the hill to the barn to be milked. One day in the 1940s while Douglas was off to war, my cousin Mary Jane and I were playing behind the house when we heard shouting. It was Uncle Elond carrying Aunt Cassie up the hill in his arms.

"Run to Ewart's and get a car," he shouted. "Cassie's been snake bit."

She had been helping Uncle Elond get up the cows and when she saw one of them coming too close, about to trample her, she had stepped backwards. In doing so she trapped a copperhead between her and the tree. He struck her on the heel. Uncle Elond ripped his shirt and made a tourniquet, then with his knife cut the wound and sucked the poison from it. He then lifted her body and carried her out of the woods, her heel bleeding profusely.

My father drove her to the doctor in Ripley as fast as he could on the winding and hilly gravel roads. Her foot was swollen and very discolored for several days, but she suffered no lasting effects. That episode dramatized for us kids the meaning of the admonition we heard every time we went outside: "Watch for snakes."

In Uncle Elond and Aunt Cassie's later years, Douglas visited several times a week regardless of how busy he was in his job. He would rather lose sleep than not see his parents to reassure them that he was always available to them.

Aunt Cassie was obsessive about having fresh vegetables, particularly tomatoes, so for several years, Douglas planted and maintained a vegetable garden she could see from the front porch. This allowed Aunt Cassie to supervise the weeding from her cane-bottom rocker.

One year, Douglas planted forty-three tomato plants just for his two parents, explaining to me for the thousandth time his tomato philosophy, "Jimmy, the point is that a slice of a tomato should be big enough to cover a slice of bread. If not, then that tomato's only good for juice."

In the mid-1960s, Douglas' work with the Neighborhood Youth Corps had a great impact on his parents. Neither quite understood the work but they knew about the integrated NYC classroom and they knew there were plenty of people in the county who didn't like it. Aunt Cassie, as usual, didn't have much to say. Uncle Elond, however, could see the handwriting on the wall.

He was not in favor of integrating the schools, but he knew it was coming whether he liked it or not. He also was influenced by Douglas' work with African Americans and he shared with Douglas his disgust with the violence directed at black people during the "Mississippi summer."

He said to Douglas, "I don't like the way people have come down here from up north and stirred things up, but in the legislature I made the laws, and I don't believe in breaking the law."

By that he meant that if the law mandated school integration then he would not go against it. More than that, he decided he'd get involved and help do what the law required, so he ran for and was elected to the County board of education. Subsequently he was named president of the school board, and, depending on Douglas for advice, he appointed a bi-racial committee on school integration. This group often met in his home as they deliberated on how best to oversee the integration process peacefully.

Remembering Uncle Elond's often stated rejection of integration and "mixing of the races," I was astonished when Douglas proudly told me about the meetings. I doubt that a black person had ever been inside that house before. In fact, no black people lived on that road, and I remembered when Aunt Cassie once told me that, "A nigra man walked up the road today," as if that in itself was the day's most noteworthy event.

Uncle Elond's desire for a peaceful integration may also have been intensified by the fact that his granddaughter, Douglas' daughter Becky was a student at Ashland High School.

If Uncle Everson had been angered by Douglas' work with the NYC, he was perhaps even angrier about Uncle Elond's leadership on the school board and made it his business to attend the board meetings and harass its members. At one memorable meeting, reported to me by Douglas, Uncle Elond became so frustrated by the interruptions, he jumped up and said, "Everson, I used to be able to whip your ass, and I think I can still do it." Fortunately for both of them, Uncle Elond thought better of it before he reached Uncle Everson.

The first attempt at integration of the Benton County Schools was voluntary, or "freedom of choice," the rule being that students could attend whatever school they wished. This occurred in the 1968-69 school year. Douglas' daughter Becky attended Ashland schools from first grade on, so was in high school during the integration years.

"During that freedom of choice year," she recalls, "a few black kids came but not many. It was peaceful. The black kids were treated well except by some of the, you know, what I called the trashy white kids. But I think the freedom of choice thing didn't work the way the government hoped, so the next year we had forced integration.

"It was in my junior year, and it was a big change because the schools were divided up." She explains that the Ashland high school, previously all white, became the district high school. Old Salem school, previously all black, became the middle school. These dramatic changes were to take place after the first semester of Becky's junior year so when the kids returned from Christmas break, they would be fully integrated.

During the Christmas break, Becky got a call from one of her fellow students, a senior, telling her that the principal told him to tell the white kids not to return to school after the break. She skipped the first day because, as she put it, "Daddy was afraid there might be some violence."

But it was peaceful so she returned the second day. She remembers the scene: "We were all mixed in with a bunch of black and white kids together, and I could feel tension, but we didn't have fights or anything like in some of the other schools I heard about."

A few days later, agents from the F.B.I. interviewed her, wanting to know who had called her. She was even issued a subpoena but didn't have to testify.

"I think the F.B.I. chose me because they knew of Daddy's work in the black community and knew I'd tell them the truth, and I did. I told them who called me and what he said, but I never heard anything else about it."

One of Becky's classmates, an African American girl named Glossie Terry remembers the atmosphere differently. "All of us black kids pretty much kept together and we were treated differently. In the school cafeteria, for instance, all we got was cheese and crackers, some peanut butter and milk. The white kids got a completely different meal. I don't know what the problem was, but we were not given a whole meal. As a group we'd get together and walk out of the lunchroom in protest."

For the most part, the rest of that school year continued with few problems, but the next year most of the white kids went to school somewhere else. "There had been 36 white kids in my junior class," Becky says, "but the next year only ten of us came back. So out of a class of 63 students, only ten of us were white."

She remembers one painful episode when she was a senior. "I was on the basketball team which was over seventy percent black. I remember that on trips we would stop to eat and people would refuse to serve us because we had blacks.

"I also remember going to play at one of the white bubba schools. We were threatened. After the girls' game, we had to stay in the dressing room during the boys' game. After the boys changed we all met and went divided boy/girl to the bus. We were told to put our heads down on our knees, and as we drove out the bubbas threw rocks and bottles at the bus."

So where did the other Ashland white kids go to school? Some went to other school districts with fewer blacks. Some found public schools with no black students. And some, those whose families could afford it, went to one of the "white academies," which in Benton County was "Gray's Academy."

CHAPTER FIFTEEN

~

The forced integration of the schools in Mississippi came more than a decade after the Brown v. Board of Education Supreme Court Ruling. From the time of the ruling there had been resistance of all sorts, from outright but peaceful defiance to a rebirth of Klan-like activity. Who can forget the photographs of federal marshals and soldiers on the scene in Little Rock, Arkansas, escorting African American kids to school?

All this came as a shock to me at the time. I suppose I was more naïve than I thought. When the ruling came down in May of 1954, I had just been elected editor of *The Mississippian*, the student newspaper at the University of Mississippi, also called "Ole Miss," a term from slave days referring to the matriarch of the plantation.

I'll never forget picking up the phone in the newspaper office to hear a reporter from *The New York*

Times. He wanted to know my reaction to the ruling and what I thought would happen.

I was flattered, of course. I gathered my thoughts, ready to speak for the University student body, and said, "I think people down here will respect the law and even though they don't like it will comply with it."

Boy, was I dumb.

Looking back, it's hard to admit just how clueless I was. After all, the place was called "Ole Miss" (still is), and at that time (and up until the 1980s) the unofficial, but ubiquitous, flag of the University was the Confederate battle flag, the infamous stars and bars.

I'll tell you how ubiquitous. One of my major extracurricular activities was band. I even drum-majored the band in my senior year. The football game halftime show always began in the same way: A gigantic Confederate battle flag—the Rebel flag—unfurled from the end zone and began floating across the field to the tune of "Dixie." As the flag progressed, members of the Rebel Band "dropped out" from under and behind the flag to form the letter "D," then "I," then "X" so that by the time the flag had finished its dramatic entrance across the field, the full band stood in formation, spelling the word "Dixie" while also playing the song of the same name. It was a spectacular beginning and it always put the all-white crowd into a joyous frenzy.

In my student days, there seemed always to be some debate involving race and integration. And there were students who clearly were stuck in some romantic notion of the "Old Confederacy." One fraternity even had its members dress in full-dress Confederate uniforms for its annual spring ball. The dates, of course, wore hoop skirts. Neither my friends nor I took any of this seriously; we thought all this was nonsense, and considered those particular fraternity members to be caricatures of themselves. In retrospect, we may have been in the minority.

The defiance and resistance to forced school integration was immediate, even though moderate voices in the business and religious and education communities were urging people to do what was best for the long term interests of the schools and students.

It turned out that a lot of folks weren't interested in moderation. It seemed that almost suddenly the state conversation was preoccupied with how to subvert public school integration. The Mississippi legislature would probably have closed all the schools if substantial business leaders and education leaders had not insisted on keeping them open.

There was fear of violence all over the state, with much of the Ku Klux Klan activity focused in the Delta, that flat rich farmland in the western part of the state along the Mississippi River. To the east, in the hills of sparsely populated Benton County, there were rumblings and a few incidents, but no real violence.

Another reaction to integration, as mentioned in chapter eleven, was the organizing of the "White Citizens' Councils" who made it their business to bring social and economic pressure against those who supported integration.

The first chapter of the WCC was, naturally, in Mississippi, organized in July of 1954, a scant two months after Brown v. Board of education. Within a few months, the WCC had attracted new chapters and members not only in Mississippi but throughout the Deep South.

I always thought that many of the "good, substantial business people," especially those who were also members of the Klan, used the WCC to camouflage their rabid racism. This became a big and influential movement, and some of its members were not shy about making life difficult for those who opposed them.

In many small towns, the groups put up signs at the city limits proclaiming, "The White Citizens Council of _____Welcomes you."

As the years passed, the WCC changed their names to things like the "Conservative Citizens Council," which seemed to give them enough legitimacy to be able to attract elected officials into their fold. But their motives and tactics remained the same.

Here are excerpts from a pamphlet from the Association of Citizens' Councils titled "Why Does Your Community Need a Citizens' Council?":

"Maybe your community has had no racial problems! This may be true; however, you may not have a fire, yet you maintain a fire department. You can depend on one thing: The NAACP (National Association for the Agitation of Colored People), aided by alien influences, bloc vote-seeking politicians and left-wing do-gooders, will see that you have a problem in the near future.

"The Citizens' Council is the South's answer to the mongrelizers. We will not be integrated. We are proud of our white blood and our white heritage of sixty centuries.

"We are certainly not ashamed of our traditions, our conservative beliefs, nor our segregated way of life."[1]

The White Citizens Councils also worked to establish a chain of private schools called "White Academies" whose sole purpose was to provide a private alternative all-white academic environment. Because the Brown

[1] Source for this material: *The Jackson Sun;* "History of the Modern Civil Rights Movement"; *The Tennessee Encyclopedia of History and Culture*

v. Board of Education ruling did not apply to private schools, the creation of segregated academies was a way to keep segregation intact.

So, in Benton County, about the time of the forced integration, Gray's Academy was established. It was successful in drawing white kids away from the public high school. It survived through 2001, and according to the classmates.com website there are still at least 68 active alums who stay in touch and have reunions.

It is obvious that these "academies" would have to charge tuition, the upshot of which was that only the higher and middle income white people could afford to send their children. The lower income white kids stayed in public schools if in any school at all.

Douglas tried through his work with the NYC to reach out to many of these families to persuade them to keep their kids in the public school. I saw him near tears once after a white man with five children told Douglas he had decided to give them no schooling at all rather than have them go to school with blacks.

Most of the white academies struggled financially, many failed, but some survived and prospered. They generally took one of two tracks: they stuck with being private secular schools or they became "Christian schools." The irony of attaching the word "Christian" to a blatantly discriminatory institution apparently escaped them.

But there is even a contemporary irony to all this. In order to maintain their tax-exempt status as non-profits, the academies were forced to integrate. Strangely enough, integration is no longer an issue at any of these schools. Many of these Christian academies have become mainstream schools in their communities and now admit any student who is qualified and has the tuition money, including a hefty percentage of African American students.

In the popular vernacular of a few years ago, Go Figure.

CHAPTER SIXTEEN

The years since being released from prison had been difficult for Douglas. Even after receiving a full pardon, he was not satisfied that he had regained his good name in the eyes of many of the citizens in Benton County. He was successful with the Neighborhood Youth Corps, but while he had become trusted and respected in the African American community, he knew that many white people felt he was a tool of the federal government and was thus not to be trusted. And of course there were those like Uncle Everson and his buddies who thought that Douglas had become too cozy with the blacks.

Although Uncle Elond's family, along with Elizabeth and her family, blamed Johnny Farese for the whole embezzlement episode, Douglas knew they'd been hurt by his conviction and imprisonment, and he felt responsible for what they'd been put through, the blank stares, the dirty looks, the surreptitious comments, the taunting of Becky by other kids.

Other things were on his mind as well. He had wanted to be an educator. He believed education to be the key to solving the race problems in the county and the South, and he wanted to be part of that. But the possibility of a role in public school education had been destroyed along with his reputation.

He believed that if he'd been able to remain superintendent of education he could have made the school integration process work better, particularly with his father on the school board. He felt he could have prevented the exodus of white kids from the schools.

Douglas had given up all hope of ever returning to any leadership position as an educator until after a few years with the NYC. His successes in the job revealed to him the possibility that he could do more, that he could once again aspire to a position of community leadership.

It had been a long road from when he was first released from prison and simply wanted to put his head down, work hard on his father-in-law's farm and in the café, and just quietly mind his own business. At that point, he had just wanted to feel normal.

But by 1970, he and Walter Webber had seen how their classes made a difference for the NYC kids, even preparing some of them for success in college. It became a testimony to Douglas of the power of education, even for young people who didn't think they were interested in education.

His appetite was whetted to return to a position in education. But how? More important, how would people accept him? Would they accept him at all? Douglas knew that he would not be able to get a job in school administration under the current county superintendent. After all, why would a superintendent risk hiring an ex-con?

He decided there was only one choice: declare his candidacy in the upcoming election for county superintendent, the job to which he had been elected 20 years before and a position that many people thought, and perhaps would still think, he had abused and dishonored. It seemed almost foolhardy on the face of it to think about running again.

But there was another factor, perhaps the deciding factor in favor of seeking the job again. His African American colleagues in the Community Action Program, as well as other leaders of the black community, urged him to seek the job. Apparently his work with the NYC was all the evidence they needed of his abilities and his integrity.

He knew he could not make the decision, however, without getting Elizabeth's agreement and full support.

The whole process of a political campaign, the predictable mud-slinging and name-calling, and the risk of re-opening old emotional wounds could be very hard on her and Becky.

Elizabeth admits she had her doubts and was fearful not only for his safety but for the hurt and rejection he might feel if he lost by a large margin. She worried that he would feel unforgiven and that his conviction would always be held against him.

She saw his determination, however, and knew that there was more at stake for him than just winning an election. She says that he really didn't expect to be elected, but he needed to know if anyone would vote for him. She promised to support him whatever he decided.

"Lib," he told her, "I'm not going to spend any money on the election. I'm just going to put my name on the ballot, talk to people and ask them to vote for me. When it's over, at least I'll know how many folks are willing to give me another chance."

So in 1971, he threw his hat in the ring. The campaign itself was an eye-opener for him as he campaigned in the African American community and among poor white people. In the 1951 campaign, he'd not spent much effort with those groups, as had no politician, except those offering to pay money for votes.

In 1971, however, he got an up-close look at how much poverty there was among those folks, how inadequate their housing, how obvious their health problems.

"All this broke Douglas' heart," Elizabeth says. "He once told me about seeing black children with what looked like white dust around their mouths. It turned out they were eating corn starch because they were so hungry. Almost every day he'd come home and report that he'd taken food to some family or given them money. And we didn't have all that much money ourselves.

"And," she adds quickly, "this was not about getting votes. This was just about Douglas."

The only money Douglas spent in the campaign was for gas and for the food and assistance he gave to those families. He still had the NYC job at the time, so he didn't even have time to campaign very hard.

He lost by only 200 votes, which convinced him that he had been redeemed in the eyes of his neighbors. The night of that loss was the very night he resolved to run again, and next time to do it right.

Chapter Seventeen

In September of 1972, Douglas received yet another affirmation of his acceptance back into the greater community. He was appointed Acting Project Director of the Corinth Community Development, Inc. This gave him even more public visibility in more communities in the area, plus the opportunity to talk about the value of education.

Here at last was the chance to talk about how an educated and skilled workforce could attract industry; about how more income could help families and the county, and yes, how that would help equalize the tax burden. In other words, he was able to campaign for the next election without really campaigning.

When 1975 came, Douglas had already identified himself with the importance of education, and this became the platform of his vigorous campaign for superintendent of education.

In the meantime, things were not going all that well in the integrated schools. Parents of both races were complaining. The black parents thought their kids weren't being given a fair chance by the white teachers. The white parents complained about the skill level of the black teachers.

I heard some of the children on the square after school ridiculing how the black teachers pronounced certain words: "Teacher told me she was gonna axe me a question." Another one said that one of her teachers told her to "close the doh," and that she counted "one, two, three, foh." These reports were met with serious head-shaking by the adults, plus the recurring comments about how integration was ruining their way of life and destroying the schools, and so on.

Some of the white people, of course, were looking for reasons why integration would not work, and many of the complaints were about how the educational standards for their children were being lowered.

The sad reality was that the standards were being lowered. Part of the problem was that, with few exceptions, the better students went to school elsewhere. Part of the problem was inadequate teacher preparation. And part of the problem was financial. There had never been enough money for education in the county, or in the state for that matter, and until the Brown v. Board of

Education decision, the concept of "separate but equal" schools had been the prevailing model.

What that really meant was that the white schools got the giant portion of the money, and the black schools got what was left. These decisions were in the hands of the county superintendent and the school board.

Douglas had explained all this to me in the 1950s when he was Superintendent. He told me how appalled he'd been by the condition of the black schools, "but," he said, "there's not much I can do about it at this point."

He explained that, "In our public schools, we are reaping the fruits of more than half a century of institutionalized racism. We white people have done everything we can to keep blacks in piss-poor schools. We didn't give them good buildings or anything else.

"Hell, I do as much as I can without getting too much attention. I give them the hand-me-down books from the white schools. Otherwise they wouldn't have had any to speak of."

I know that these memories of twenty years earlier were still plaguing Douglas during his campaign of 1975. His overriding campaign promise was to increase the quality of public education in the county. He knew it would not be easy and he knew where he would have to begin: with the teachers.

He told me, "You won't believe this, Jimmy, but we have teachers with master's degrees who can't pass an eighth grade equivalency test."

"How did that happen?" I asked.

"We've been stacking the system against the blacks for a long time. We pass them right on through middle school and high school, and those who want to go to college have to go to all-black schools."

"I thought they were okay," I said.

"Some of them are, but most of them are not. Where do they get their faculty? Most of them come from our schools and from colleges where they probably didn't get beyond a high school education themselves. So it just continues downward. Meanwhile, they get degrees and on paper have all the qualifications."

"So when the forced integration came…."

"You got it, all the teachers were integrated and were assigned schools and classes based on their academic records."

"What are you going to do if you're elected?"

"Don't get me wrong, not all the black teachers are inadequate by any means. Some of them have good experience and are good teachers." He laughed. "Even though they might use their own pronunciation for some words. You know, that's funny as hell considering all the speaking problems that we white people have down here.

"I can work with a lot of those teachers. But let me tell you that we have some bad white teachers too, some of whom have been at it a long time and are still teaching what they taught twenty-five years ago. But they're somebody's cousin or aunt or mother-in-law and it's hard to get rid of them."

"But you will?"

"I wish I could say that but I can't. It's almost impossible to fire teachers of either race, but I'll have the same standards and expectations for both black and white, and I'll be clear about what constitutes good teaching and what doesn't. I'll say that."

The campaign was hard-fought, though Douglas never talked about his opponents but just stuck to what he wanted to do for education in the county. The newspapers reported later that none of Douglas' opponents brought up his conviction or prison time.

"I don't believe that," Becky recalls. "I heard one of them, or maybe it was one of their supporters, call Daddy an S.O.B and say they couldn't understand how anyone could vote for a crook."

In the town of Ashland, it became apparent to some that people revealed how they were going to vote by where they shopped and with whom they talked.

The Rev. William Kemp, a retired Methodist minister and good friend of Douglas and Elizabeth, said, "I could stand on the courthouse lawn and just look around the square. Based on where people stopped, what stores they went in, which café they chose, and so on, I could tell exactly how they were going to vote. I could tell which ones were with Douglas and which ones were against him."

What became clear is that the African American community was solidly behind Douglas. They had gotten to know him well during the Neighborhood Youth Corps days, and they trusted him and knew he would be fair. He'd had their votes in the 1971 elections, and several of the black leaders urged him to run again and pledged their support.

I can only speculate about his support by the white people. I think many of them felt he had been railroaded into prison and agreed with Willie Ruth Daugherty that he "took the rap" for others. I was also told that many white people knew that Douglas had the trust of the black leaders, thus would have the support he needed to crack down on the black teachers. I'm not sure the white people knew he also planned to crack down on the white teachers. His would be an equal-opportunity crack down.

CHAPTER EIGHTEEN

"Benton Voters Give Ex-Official New Chance As Superintendent"

With this headline on September 21, 1975, *The Commercial Appeal of Memphis*, one of the South's largest newspapers, announced the election of Douglas.

The newspaper credited Douglas for "living a straight life," and "gaining the confidence and forgiveness of his neighbors." It also reported that "Autry may have what few men ever have—a second chance."

The photographs show a very different Douglas Autry from the one pictured with his lawyer in the *Tupelo Journal* in 1956. The younger Douglas, only twenty-nine years old when convicted, is slim and fit though obviously exhausted and burdened physically by the emotional weight of the trial.

By 1975, Douglas' big smile was back and he was showing the weight so characteristic of the Hudspeth side of our family. He was not as big as Uncle Bob by any means, but like his father, he was "stout." He had given up cigarettes but was rarely seen without his ubiquitous thin little cigars.

The Commercial Appeal reported that Douglas had been elected with 61% of the vote. He was reluctant to talk to the reporter about the events of twenty years ago, saying only that he maintained his innocence as he had then.

He asserted that, "I haven't justified anything, except I'm capable of being elected. Understand, I've only come back part of the way. All I have now is the opportunity. My big day will be when I come out of the superintendent's office and they say, 'You've done a good job.'"

When asked why he decided to seek the job again, he said he wanted to prove he could do a good job.

"I'm not apologetic," he said. "I'm a competent person. If I didn't think I was, I wouldn't run for superintendent.

"I'm a grandfather now. You realize you want your children and grandchildren to hear good things about you."

Thus, in a way, Douglas started all over again and would go on to be elected two more times and to serve an unprecedented three terms, from 1976 to 1988.

It did not take long in that first term for Douglas to signal that things were going to change.

In fact, they began to change even before he officially took over. One of his daughter's schoolmates, an African American girl named Glossie Terry, was an employee of Douglas' predecessor, working in one of the department's satellite offices in which a federal program was being administered. The federally funded programs mandated the hiring of African Americans; otherwise, she suggests, she probably would not have been there.

She remembers that, at the time of Douglas' predecessor's departure, the staff had a Christmas party. "But I was not invited."

"You think it was racial?" I asked.

"Of course," she said. "They didn't even tell me about it but Mr. Autry found out about it and called me and asked was I invited? I told him no, I didn't know anything about it. So he called one of the senior staff people and asked why was I not invited. So that person came to me and said they just hadn't got around to telling me, and all that. You know, making excuses.

"You see, we had already formed a relationship and he was still looking out for me." Glossie recalled a few years earlier, while Douglas was still with the NYC and before he'd even decided to run again for Superintendent, she was passed over for a raise. "The board voted for everybody's else in the department to get a raise. Except me."

"Racial?" I asked.

"Definitely. At the time, everybody in the black community knew that Mr. Autry was the go-to guy if you needed help. When I told him, he called some members of the school board. They voted again and I got the raise."

Glossie had known Douglas from the time she was given summer jobs with the NYC, and she was delighted that he'd been elected. "With Mr. Autry in charge, you felt like you belonged, you felt like you contributed. In the previous administration, I felt like they just had to have a black in a position and I was it. A token. I was just given a paycheck, answering the phone, and doing whatever else I was told.

"With Mr. Autry, it was a totally different atmosphere. You were assigned a job and he expected you to do it. You didn't lax off and not do your job just because he was in office. None of that. You had to do your job. But you didn't mind. It's a difference when you don't mind doing your job.

"And it was fun. Mr. Autry was a lot of fun. You know, we all did the budgets together. We'd sit around a big table with Coca Colas and sandwiches and work, then we'd joke and laugh, then we'd work some more. He was a lot of fun. He liked to laugh."

Glossie also said that everyone knew he would advocate for them, black or white. "If you had a problem, you knew you could go to Mr. Autry, and if he couldn't solve it, he'd help you find somebody who could. He was the most open-minded white person I ever knew."

She told me that, unlike other superintendents of education, Douglas would not ride to conferences and meetings in a separate car. He always rode with his staff. This prompted a particularly intense memory for her.

On one trip, the group stopped for lunch in Kosciusko. When they sat down in the restaurant, the proprietor came to their table and said, "We can't serve her," pointing to Glossie. Douglas stood up and said, "We all get served or none of us gets served." To which Glossie added, "Let's just get out of here."

I asked Glossie the question I asked everyone I interviewed, "What do you know about Douglas' trial and conviction back in the 1950s?"

"I was too young to know anything about it then, but my parents and my father-in-law told me about it."

"What did they think?"

"Well, they loved Mr. Autry and they said he was made a scapegoat."

CHAPTER NINETEEN

~

Ann Bean, another African American, was a fellow student of Becky's and Glossie's in Ashland High School in the year after the forced integration. Douglas was impressed with her and after graduation hired her to work in the Neighborhood Youth Corps, by then known as the CETA program (Community Employment Training Act). Later, when he decided to run for the superintendent's job, he asked her if she wanted to come to work for him if he won.

"I was flattered, but I didn't think a lot about it. I was sure he would probably say things like that to a lot of people." But after the campaign, he contacted her at her office job with the Sunbeam company in Holly Springs and offered her a job in the superintendent's office.

Thus Ann Bean (now Ann Luellen) became the first African American in history to work in an office of the

Benton County Courthouse. This in itself could have been very intimidating.

"At first," Ann says, "I was concerned about going there. I thought, 'I'm the first African American, we said black at that time, person to work here, surrounded by whites and no other black people'....yes I was nervous about it. But once in the job, Mr. Autry made everything all right. He'd come in and ask me, 'Everything all right?' I'd say yes, then he would ask my white co-workers, 'Everything all right?' With him there, I became very comfortable."

When I asked Ann how her co-workers treated her, she said, "Fine." Then she added that "after a while, one of them said she just didn't realize that black people were, you know, like I was."

I asked Ann what she thought her co-worker meant by that. "It wasn't a compliment but I guess it depends on how you look at it. I think what she meant was that she had always looked down on black people, and after she had the opportunity to work with me she got to know that African Americans were not beneath her.

"Yes, it was negative in a sense, but I took it as more that she just hadn't had an opportunity to work with people of my color."

As for other people in the courthouse, they were cordial. "Nobody made me feel uncomfortable. When they'd come into the superintendent's office they'd speak and were friendly but I didn't really get very close to any of them."

Ann believes that Douglas was the key to her acceptance at the courthouse. When I told her I thought she'd been very brave to take the job and walk into that courthouse every day, given the atmosphere at the time, she responded, "I just appreciated the opportunity that Mr. Autry gave me to have that experience."

I asked the question I asked many people in Benton County: "How do you think Douglas developed such a sensitivity to poor people, both black and white? After all, he was a white Mississippi farm boy like so many others."

Ann replied, "I truly think he was a man who just didn't see color; he saw people as people. He didn't see red or white or green or whatever, but at that time it was just black and white. He just didn't see it. He was very compassionate. I never saw him treat one person different from another, African American or white. And I think that made him able to work with the teachers and students of both races and to solve a lot of problems."

Ann experienced a little bit of history repeating itself when she was part of an episode eerily similar to the one Glossie had gone through. The situation was the same, a staff driving trip.

"We were going to a conference and stopped for lunch at a restaurant in Granada. After we sat there a while, a man came up and said to Mr. Autry that we can't serve her here."

This restaurant was yet another example of how individual businesses flouted the integration order. Ann said she was hurt and embarrassed by the episode but she didn't speak out. "I knew Mr. Autry would take care of it."

"This isn't the only place to eat," Douglas told the man. "If you can't serve her you can't serve any of us." He and his staff stood and walked out. Later at the hotel in Jackson, Ann recalls that the group was having refreshments in the bar. When she excused herself to return to her room, Douglas made sure she got there safely. "I think he walked with me because I was the only African American person in the bar, and he wanted me to not be harassed. When he saw that I was safe, he went back to the group."

Ann got married in 1978. She delighted in telling me that her white co-workers came to the wedding. After commuting from Memphis for three years, she finally found a job there in 1981 and reluctantly resigned from the county superintendent's office.

Now she seems to place no special importance on having made history in the Benton County courthouse. But, together with Douglas, she made history nonetheless.

Chapter Twenty

~

Spence Richards, an African American, now 87 years old, who worked in maintenance for the Holly Springs school system for many years, thinks he found the papers that could have kept Douglas out of jail. Unfortunately, he doesn't remember what they showed and doesn't know how they could have helped Douglas. He only knows what Douglas said when shown the papers.

Spence explained, that "I was working in Holly Springs at the time. This was when Mr. Autry was working for that youth corps program, or something like that, about 1969 or 1970. I had to go into a building right next to where the gasoline truck that took gas to the school buses came to fill up. I went into the basement and when I looked around I saw a hole in the wall where there had been an old flue. It looked like there was some papers stuck up in there. So I got something to stand on and fished them out.

"The papers were so old they was almost rotten. I looked at them and I saw Mr. Autry's name and the names of some of the people I knew had been on the school board in Benton County. Later I saw Mr. Autry and just mentioned the papers and asked if he'd like to see them.

"He said he sure would, that he believed he knew what they might be. So when I brought them to him, he looked at them a long time and he finally said, 'Mr. Richards, these are the papers. If I could have found these papers, they would have kept me out of prison. I asked the courthouse janitor and everybody I could think of, and I have no idea how those papers got from my office to that building in Holly Springs.'"

I asked Spence what he thought the papers might have been. "I'm not sure because it wasn't any of my business but I did see something about delivering gas, and the papers looked like they were supposed to be headed for Mr. Autry's office. And somebody had told me there was supposed to be some papers headed for the superintendent's office that never made it and everybody in the office had searched for them but couldn't find them."

After all these years, it's impossible to piece together what they may have been and how they might have helped Douglas' case. It remains a mystery with too many unanswerable questions to pursue: Why would someone have hidden them instead of just burning them? Or were they just lost, dropped by accident?

There are no answers except from Spence, who remains suspicious that they were part of the way that Douglas got set up and sent to prison.

A few years later, after the files were found, when Douglas needed a maintenance person in the Ashland schools, he hired Spence who worked in Holly Springs but lived in Ashland and had told Douglas he'd like to work closer to home and avoid the commute.

He and Douglas struck up a close working relationship that was to last for the full three terms of Douglas' tenure.

"I never worked with or knew a finer person, black or white," Spence told me. "We were together all those years and never got any more crossways than you and I are right now."

Spence recalls a time when some of the white people in the community were complaining about the condition of the schools and scheduled a meeting to discuss their complaints. Douglas asked him to attend the meeting and listen.

"So I just stood in the back, and these people were going on and on about this and that and grumbling. Finally one of the ladies said, 'There's Spence Richards over there. Maybe he's got something to say.'

"So I went in there and stood at some kind of little thing that looked like a pulpit and said, 'Hello everybody. I understand that y'all see the school in bad shape, but I don't see it quite as bad as y'all are making it sound like it is. But I'll tell you what. You name me some priorities that y'all see that need to be done quickly and I'll get them done.' Then the head man of the committee said, 'Paint that square back up on the basketball goal.'

"You see, somebody had painted the basketball goal white and hadn't painted the square behind the basket. Now that man that was going on and on about how bad the school was, called that a priority in the school system. Shoot. I thought he'd name bad restrooms or leaks or broken windows or something that was a real priority. I wondered what are these folks really up here for?

"I said to myself, 'I may have been born in the dark, but it wasn't last night.' I know what a priority is and it isn't a square on the basketball goal. They said some other nit-picking things.

"They were trying to cook up some trouble for Mr. Autry. He heard about it and the next morning he came to the school where I sign in and he said, 'Mr. Richards,

I got your message and heard what you said at the meeting. You came out with flying colors.'

"Mr. Autry knew some people didn't like him but he never let that bother him. When he heard somebody didn't like him, he'd go directly to them and try to talk about it."

Spence remembers being in the thick of the civil rights movement. When the voter registration drive began, and northerners came to assist in voter registration, they asked Spence to be a test case.

"I was picked out to be picked on," he says. "They had a place in the post office to show people how to register to vote. There was a white man who lived close to me who couldn't read and write and he had been allowed to vote.

"They took him and me down there to Oxford, to the Federal building or something like that, and they put me right in the middle of this court. They asked me what grade I finished school in. I said, 'Eighth grade and a little into the ninth and that's where I stopped.' Then they got this white man up there, and he had gone to school from slight to none.

"They asked him if he could vote and he said he'd been voting for years. Then they asked me, 'Spence, have you voted?' I said, 'No, because I got to pass this literacy test or something like that.'"

Spence paused in his story and said to me, "Mr. Autry, I knew how it worked. The blacks were last hired, first fired. It's better now, but I knew what was going on then. When Martin Luther Junior marched over there in Alabama, I liked what he said and all that. But look, I also could understand why white people didn't like what they heard."

He recalled when the Little Rock schools were integrated. He said that he and the Holly Springs school superintendent watched television coverage of the black children being escorted to school, and the superintendent told him, "Spence, it won't be long before black and white children are going to the same school together here."

Spence responded that he wouldn't live long enough to see that, and the school superintendent said, "You better die soon then, Spence, because it's on its way."

About fifteen years later, Spence's daughter was one of four black students, including Glossie Terry and Ann Luellen, who integrated the Ashland high school. This was in the first year of integration by choice, before the next year's forced integration.

A lot of black people didn't want the integration. They were scared of it.

"Lunch in the lunchroom cost a quarter," Spence says. "We didn't have no money, so my daughter's grandmother was paying for her lunch. But she stopped paying the quarter to try to make us stop sending her to the school. But we kept doing it.

"Times were hard," he said. "During the week we ate canned salmon and spaghetti, then on Sunday, for variety, we ate spaghetti and canned salmon." He laughed.

For a while during those years, Spence had some tension with his white neighbors. One night someone burned a cross on the road between his house and a neighbor; on another occasion, a white man in a pickup truck blocked the road, then left his truck and walked casually over to another white man who'd been working in a field, and began to talk.

"I didn't try to drive around his truck or anything." Spence said, "I just waited until he got in his truck. Then when he took off he spun his tires and threw gravel up on my car. I just went on. I didn't say nothing."

I asked if he was scared sometimes.

"Not really scared but worried," he said. "I came close to buying a pistol one time, but I figured no pistol could stop them if they wanted to kill me."

He talked again about Douglas, telling me, "He was a man who believed in justice for everybody and who accepted everybody. I can't say that about some of the people around here."

The conversation turned to President Obama. I asked Spence how he felt about Obama's election.

He paused a long time, then talked a while about the history of slavery, and concluded, "Hey look, we done had a hard time, but we're slowly turning out to be some important folks."

Chapter Twenty-One

Douglas knew he'd have to be extra careful, even on guard, as he came into the superintendent's job for the second time. Although he was elected by an overwhelming majority, there remained many white people in the county who were opposed to his election. Some of them just didn't want an "ex-con" in the job of educating our children. Others felt he'd make it too easy on the blacks and too hard on the whites.

Douglas knew, too, that there were several different reasons that his white supporters had voted for him. Some genuinely liked him, felt he has been unfairly convicted and deserved another chance. There were others who didn't know him well but knew he had taken the rap for others and felt somewhat ashamed that they had not supported him at the time. Then there were white people who voted for him not because they thought he'd do a good job but because they felt that, as the only white person whom the black community trusted, he'd be able to "keep the blacks in line."

He knew he would not be able to fulfill everyone's expectations, but he vowed to do what he could to help all the students in the county. "If I stick to just improving education for the students and keeping the peace in the schools, those are the most important things I can do," he told me.

He knew also, as does anyone who has been elected to public office that, more often than not, it's not the major policy changes you make so much as the everyday things you do that mean success or failure, because it's the everyday things that have the greatest impact on the public's perception.

Douglas was particularly careful about any matter involving public funds. He had used his time in the NYC well, learning to identify and comply with the myriad bureaucratic rules governing how public money was to be handled. Everyone in the school system understood his iron-clad rule: Everything in the budget had to be spent as budgeted.

Becky remembers this as one of his daily anxieties. Part of the worry, she said, was that there might be those, including political adversaries as well as the racist elements like the Klan, who would try to create the impression that he was, "up to his old tricks."

"One time in the lunch room," Becky told me, "some money was missing. It wasn't a big amount, but Daddy got on top of that quickly. Turned out someone had stolen the money and it was never found. But Daddy quickly reported the incident to the appropriate authorities.

"And a good thing, too, because some lady had written a letter to the state department of education saying that Daddy was stealing money from the little children. The department sent Daddy a copy of the letter, but they didn't do anything about it."

There was fear among some of the white people that Douglas was going to, in Becky's words, "push blacks on them." One man said, "That nigger lover Douglas is going to see to it that they get things before the whites." By that time, the Ashland school was about 85% black.

No one would confront Douglas directly with these kinds of accusations and comments, so there was little response he could make but to continue to do his job very carefully.

He told me in those years that everybody was "coming at me from all sides."

"Including the blacks?" I asked.

"Oh yes. I haven't done nearly what the NAACP wants me to do. I think most of the blacks here know that I am going to do everything I can for them, and they know they'll get their fair share of everything. But the NAACP is always pushing me. The problem is that I generally agree with them, but they can't seem to understand that we're in a transition and I'm going as far as I can and still keep things on an even keel."

On top of the racial unrest, Douglas faced the perennial problem of all public schools: resources. There simply was not enough money to bring the county schools up to a reasonable standard.

"We're not talking about making the Benton County schools the best in the nation, or even in the state. I just need to make them so that all our students can graduate with a diploma that means something. As it is now, many of our graduates can just barely get by."

Douglas decided to try to get a bond issue passed. He campaigned as the spokesman for the students saying all the money would be designated to improve the schools. It's never easy to get a bond issue passed anywhere, but Douglas was stunned by the viciousness of the attacks on him personally rather than on the issue itself. The people opposing the bonding dredged up all the details of his earlier conviction, despite his having received a full pardon. One man bought radio ads saying that Douglas would steal the money from the bond issue, that he would, in effect, be taking money from the kids. All this was reminiscent of the prosecuting attorney's accusation twenty-five years earlier that Douglas had stolen food and books from the students.

The Klan burned a cross in a black man's yard. But those activities didn't get far. The FBI came and conducted an investigation and the cross-burning stopped. Douglas commented that "some of those birds in Everson's group were walking a tightrope for a while."

The bond issue did not pass.

I visited Douglas regularly during this time and was always impressed by his equanimity in the midst of it all.

"How do you stayed focused, and how do you decide what to do every day?" I asked him.

"Hell, Jimmy," he answered, "I learned to focus when I was shooting at Kamikazes, and if you don't stay focused in prison you go out of your mind. Most of the time in this job, it's not hard. I try to keep my attention on the kids and the teachers."

Even that was not without its problems, not the least of which was either the unwillingness or inability of some key staff members to support him. Douglas once complained to me that the principal "hides in his office and seems to be afraid to try to solve the problems. Hell, in some ways I don't blame him. He's caught between the blacks and whites, but it's his job and he's supposed to do it."

But when there were incidents or threats of unrest by students, it was Douglas who most often had to show up at the school and act on behalf of the principal to impose discipline. Some of the black students were determined to test the system generally and Douglas specifically. So they pushed him. But Douglas would only be pushed so far. In one seminal confrontation, a young black man refused to go to class and was disrupting the school with his behavior. When he raised his voice to Douglas, Douglas picked him up by the collar, backed him into a wall, and gave him a lecture on respect, then said, "Mr. _____, you will get back into that classroom and you will stop causing trouble." The young man returned to class.

I told Becky that, these days, that kind of action by a school official would probably bring some kind of reprimand or lawsuit or both.

"I think the reason Daddy could do that," she said, "is because the black parents trusted him to treat their kids fairly. They knew that he wanted what was best for them."

Douglas did all he could to assure that blacks were getting their share of everything, but there was always the risk of creating a controversy. Early in his tenure, the black community leaders expressed their dislike and distrust of a white co-principal at one of the schools. Then they went to the school board with their complaint.

There was no public protest, and the school board meeting was not disrupted, but Douglas knew that if he did not do something about their concerns, there would be a major problem. So he did not renew the co-principal's contract. Of course this brought criticism from his white critics that he was favoring the blacks over the whites.

Uncle Everson, who would not even speak to Douglas any more, told anyone who would listen that he thought it was "a hell of a note that a bunch of niggers can get a white man fired."

But Douglas never seemed upset by the names he was called. "If those sorry old boys call me a 'nigger lover,' then I must be doing something right," he told me.

CHAPTER TWENTY-TWO

~

I have often described Douglas as the most generous person I've ever known. If he could find a way to say yes to anyone in need, he would. This generous and trusting nature may have been a factor in the legal problems of his first term as Superintendent of Education, but it was also his most defining and endearing characteristic.

Becky recalled that she could remember her father seeing "children who needed shoes or coats or whatever, and he would go out and buy and take them to their house or give the parents the money to buy whatever was needed."

"Also I remember blacks coming to our house and borrowing money from Daddy. This was probably on a weekly basis. Sometimes Daddy was paid back and sometimes not."

After his death, Elizabeth told me she hadn't realized how generous he was. "People keep coming up to me and telling me stories about how Douglas helped them, how he'd just give them money if they needed it, and so on." She paused. "And we didn't have that much money."

I have been amazed how Douglas, after his clearly fishy conviction, after the insults and threats, and in the midst of the complaints from both sides of the racial issues, was nonetheless able to bring his innate generosity into his daily work life.

Glossie Terry recalls how far Douglas would go to keep a student from being expelled. "He was like an uncle or grandfather to the staff and to the kids." She described how, when he received a report that a student was in the process of expulsion, he would often intervene, talk to the student and the parents and the teachers or principal and try to work out another chance for the kid. "He kept a lot of kids in school that way because he knew that if they dropped out or were expelled, they'd never have a good chance in life."

Becky recalls Douglas admonition to her: "Once you give your word, you keep it. And never make false promises."

"One thing about Daddy," she said, "is once he gave his word, during a campaign or any other time, he kept it. If he said 'I will' do something, he would.

"There was a woman in Hickory Flat who asked him for a job during his campaign and he said yes. When the job came available, he called her and offered it to her. The woman said, 'Oh my goodness, I thought it was just a campaign promise.'"

Becky also tells about a young woman, described as "a dwarf and slightly retarded," who told Douglas she wanted to be a teacher's aide. He told her mother, "I will give her a job as soon as I find something she can do." There was nothing available, and the mother became frustrated and angry, but "Daddy was waiting for the right job. When it came open, he gave it to the girl and she did very well in it."

Douglas' passion about education moved him and Elizabeth to pay to send a young woman to junior college. I asked Elizabeth why they did it, considering how many other young people had the same needs. "Douglas felt she had the intelligence and the ambition to rise above the situation she'd been born into, so we did it." Elizabeth gave no further explanation.

I have often wondered where Douglas' passion for education came from. Both my father and Uncle Elond taught school briefly. Perhaps that was it. Perhaps it developed while he was on the GI bill at the University of Missouri. My brother once said that it clearly was Douglas' calling. Whatever the genesis of that passion, it carried him through a career of facing what seemed a never ending series of difficult circumstances.

As the situation in the Benton County public schools moved toward stability, Douglas began to worry about the white students who had left the public schools to attend Gray's Academy.

"They don't have the materials and the books they need, Jimmy," he told me, "so I'm going to try to do something about that. I've been meeting with them."

"Douglas," I said, "a private school is not your responsibility, and you might get yourself in trouble particularly if you do anything for them that costs money."

Douglas listened and nodded. "I appreciate that, and I've thought a lot about it. But here's the thing: I have some responsibility to see that the young people of this county get an education. I include all the young people, no matter where they go to school."

"I'm not surprised that you feel that way," I answered. "In fact, I'd be surprised if you didn't feel that way. You grew up with a lot of those kids' parents and grandparents. But they chose the private school and they did it for all the wrong reasons. Why don't you just try to get them to transfer back to the public schools?"

"Some of them will and have, but it's not the kids' fault. It's their parents who can't live with the integration. The problem is it's the kids who're getting short-changed."

"But I've heard they have some good teachers over there."

"They do. It's not the teachers. It's resources."

"So what are you going to do?"

"I plan to give them some books and supplies."

"You're asking for trouble, Douglas," I said.

"Jimmy, you know damned well that with my background I'm not going to risk doing anything illegal. I plan to give them books and stuff that we'll just toss because we have new ones. And the school board will be with me all the way."

I was worried that all his old adversaries would trot out their criticisms and their "told you so's" but it didn't happen. Whatever Douglas did was accomplished very quietly, not, I suspect, because Douglas feared publicity or protest, but because he felt that the people of the private school, established to perpetuate segregation, would be embarrassed if it were known they were getting supplies from the integrated school system.

And it would not be in Douglas' generous nature to embarrass anyone.

Chapter Twenty-Three

~

Douglas had been sitting quietly for a while, then he sighed deeply, shifted in his chair, and looked at me. I thought he looked profoundly sad.

"Jimmy, the problem is the 'grandma syndrome.'"

"What are you talking about, Douglas?" I asked.

The year was 1986 and Douglas was in his final four-year term as Superintendent. I was visiting him and Elizabeth in the home they had built on the ground we called "the old place," where the birthplace of my father and his had stood before it burned. We'd been talking about snake dogs, having just finished a dinner of Elizabeth's fried chicken, field peas, creamed corn, corn bread, sliced fresh tomatoes from the garden, and peach cobbler. He was pulling on one of the thirty or so little thin cigars he smoked every day, claiming they were helping him stop smoking cigarettes.

One of the family had a toddler there, sitting on the floor looking out a sliding glass door at Douglas' beloved beagles. The toddler slapped his open hand against the glass.

Douglas turned his attention to the dogs and said, "Hey, Boomer, Come on over here, old boy." He made that sucking, clicking sound everyone makes calling a dog. Boomer came to the door.

"Half basset, half beagle. Look at those ears and the way his front feet splay out."

The toddler pushed his hand against the door, and the dog tried to sniff it through the glass.

"Old Boomer is peculiar, pretty much of a loner. Those other dogs will jump a rabbit and take off in one direction, and Boomer will find himself another rabbit and take off in the other direction by himself. And he has the coldest nose you ever saw. He can smell up a spot where a rabbit spent the night, then trail him up, opening every step of the way."

Douglas then looked far off, the way everyone in the family seems to do from time to time, as if searching in the trees somewhere for some kind of answer to something, neither the question nor the answer ever directly stated.

So I asked him again what he was talking about, knowing it wasn't snake dogs or beagle hounds.

"Well, I guess I have to say that I'm having more trouble with black students than I've ever had." He paused. "I mean, shit, it just isn't worth it sometimes."

"I don't think I've ever seen you like this," I said, then asked, "What did you mean by the 'grandma syndrome?'"

"Well, you know what happened after World War Two. Blacks down here heard from some of the veterans about the good jobs up north. And they heard there wasn't any segregation up there. Now you and I know there's a lot of bullshit in that, but the treatment in the north certainly was better than down here. So blacks headed north by the thousands. And that included a lot of Benton County blacks."

"I knew about the migration but I didn't think it had much effect here."

"It's all relative. A lot of our young black people left for Chicago and Detroit and Cleveland. They went for the jobs. There sure as hell wasn't anything down here for them to do. The veterans especially weren't happy here. They'd had a lot of freedom in the military and they didn't want to come back to this 'Yassa Boss, step off the sidewalk when the white man walks by' crap.

"So they cleared out. And a lot of them did well up there. They'd drive their big new cars down here to visit, then more of their friends and family would follow them when they left."

He paused.

"I'm not following you, Douglas. What does this have to do with your students?"

"Simple. Many of these blacks who now live up north find themselves in rough neighborhoods. They are afraid their kids are going to join gangs and get killed or go to jail. They remember their Mississippi roots. They remember the good times. Despite the racism, they remember a childhood that was happy and safe."

"Well, we all tend to look back through rose-colored glasses and remember the good things, not the bad things. So what?"

"So just this: they get to thinking how nice it would be if their own kids could experience this wholesome, crime-free environment, and they say to themselves, 'Let's send junior down home and let Grandma raise him.'"

"Really?" I asked, "Is there much of that?"

"You'd be surprised. But here's the problem: Junior doesn't leave his knives and guns and drugs behind. He brings them with him. And of course, there are plenty of knives and guns down here, but I never saw them in school before."

Douglas grimaced, shook his head, and lit another little cigar. "I've had to break up more fights in the past couple of years than in all my years in the job, including the first time. So far, no one has been hurt seriously, but I worry that it's just a matter of time."

Boomer was whining at the door much to the delight of the toddler.

"He wants to go hunting, don't you, Boomer?" Douglas asked. The dog wagged his tail and another dog, a terrier, came to the door.

"That's Trixie," Douglas said. "She's my snake dog."

"You have a lot of snakes here?"

"Lord yes," said Elizabeth. There are big cottonmouths down there in the creek and they come up around here sometimes."

"And you should watch Trixie then," Douglas interrupted. "She will grab that snake behind the head before he can strike, and shake him dead in one quick jerk of her head."

He clucked at Trixie. "Won't you girl? We need a dog like that around this place. And she'll also tree squirrels."

I waited until Douglas looked at me again. "So what are you going to do?"

"I'm not sure. It's a new kind of violence for us and to my mind it sets back some of the progress we've made. It's like this whole racial thing is just relentless. It just grinds on."

"So," I asked again, 'What are you going to do?"

"Same thing I've been doing," I guess. "Just try to keep the peace and help the kids get an education.

Chapter Twenty-Four

~

Though some do it grudgingly, most of the people in Benton County—that is, those who remember—will agree that Douglas did keep the peace, that he did improve the schools, and that he was a champion for education.

The high schools are well integrated now. Though Gray's Academy no longer exists there are other academies in the state, most of which began as "white academies" but have now become "Christian academies." Ironically, they too are integrated. The whole subject of race is mostly a non-issue for the younger generation, though it would be naïve to suggest that racism is not still well entrenched in Mississippi.

As for Douglas, he retired after his third term in 1988, having served for twelve years. He was recognized and honored throughout the retirement process as a champion for students. The board of trustees at Northwest Mississippi Community College, on whose board he served, passed a special resolution of commendation for his "distinct and lasting contribution to education both in his own community and in the State of Mississippi."

Douglas accepted the recognition with his usual modesty and good humor and seemed not to make too much of it. He agreed with my father that honorary degrees and resolutions of commendation were "just so much curl in a pig's tail." But I know Douglas felt he had fully redeemed himself in the eyes of the community.

In the early eighties he had become very engaged with the genealogy of the family and had corresponded with Autry relatives around the country. He organized the rest of us to contribute to a large family history put together by one of our university professor kinsmen.

There were three branches of the family: Autry, Grisham, and Hudspeth. Douglas worked with representatives of each to put together family reunions every summer. Sometimes he would share the master of ceremonies duties.

These were characteristically Southern gatherings, with much gospel music singing and much reminiscing, followed by enough food to feed an army. And punctuated, always, with good-natured commentary: "Those boys are going through that fried chicken like Grant through Richmond!"

When I attended the reunions, I found myself marveling at the irony that these families could come together, seeming to ignore what I knew were vast disagreements about religion, politics, and race. And I could always feel the unspoken story of Douglas' prison time and his identity as a liberal white man. But you'd never be able to detect any animosity amidst the back-slapping, laughing behavior of the men.

Douglas helped organize a campaign to raise money for a headstone to mark the grave of our forebear Jacob Autry, the Confederate soldier who after being wounded walked home and quit the war. The headstone is still there, a hundred yards from a road in the Holly Springs National Forest where he is buried.

I think the connection to family began to mean a lot more to Douglas in his later years, perhaps because of the unacknowledged split between my Dad and Uncle Elond on the one side and Everson and the sisters Ruvess and Valena on the other. Douglas felt the split probably had a lot to do with his work and his relationship with Everson.

Douglas also had great plans for his land. He planted an orchard, put in catfish ponds, and bought a few head of livestock. He could picture himself feeding and milking a cow, churning butter, and doing all the old things he'd grown up with. He even planned to experiment with raising goats, and subscribed to magazines and journals to learn the breeds and techniques for raising them.

But as he was about to retire, three of his most beloved people died. Uncle Elond died in August of 1987. Douglas' sister Lavern died in September of that year and his mother, Aunt Cassie, died the following January.

Soon after, his joints began to ache, first the shoulders, then the knees. Nothing helped. Finally he had the diagnosis: rheumatoid arthritis. He tried not to give into it for a long time, but he began a long steady decline until his death in 1996, thus his plans for gardening, milking his cow, and raising goats became an unfulfilled dream. He attributed his arthritis to the triple shock of family deaths.

"I think all that grief just played hell with my immune system," he told me many times during the years of his pain. Elizabeth was always his faithful caretaker, while those of us who had moved away could do little but stay in touch. Through it all, he maintained his country-boy sense of humor, making jokes of his inability to even go to the bathroom by himself.

Strangely enough during his last years in office and during his retirement and physical decline, Douglas became a political power in the county. Becky puts it this way: "The blacks had trusted Daddy and knew he wanted them to have a good life. They would talk to him about everything that was going on. Actually, it got to where he could get whoever he wanted elected at that time because the blacks would vote for whoever he wanted in office. He was respected but also hated for having that much influence."

So, in addition to family and friends, he had an unending stream of political visitors to his living room where he sat in an overstuffed chair and held court. Consider the irony of every aspiring politician in Benton County and much of North Mississippi making a path to Douglas' door down there at the "old place," seeking his counsel and advice, as well as his support, before running for office.

I still smile when I think about it.

Chapter Twenty-Five

~

Dear Mrs. Autry

Please accept our deepest sympathy in your loss.

We thought you and other family members would like to know that the Mississippi House of Representatives recently voted to adjourn in memory of Mr. Douglas Autry.

With kindest regards, I am

Sincerely yours,

Tim Ford

Speaker, State of Mississippi

House of Representatives

I was standing in the sun, trying to gulp back my tears, when they brought the casket out of the funeral home and down the steps, and slid it into the hearse. It was the first funeral in our family not held in the church our grandfather and my father had pastored. Elizabeth explained that Douglas refused to go back into the church except for his parents' funerals. "He just couldn't forget how the people in the congregation let him down and how many of them treated his daddy."

As the pallbearers turned away from the hearse, one of my cousins, looking at Douglas and Elizabeth's young friend Theodore Hardin, said, "Now there's something you don't usually see in these parts, a black pallbearer at a white funeral." Theodore was not only a good friend; he was an invaluable helper who had done odd jobs for Douglas and Elizabeth since he was in the tenth grade, ten years before Douglas died. As Douglas' health declined, Theodore became a major caretaker. He still takes care of the land and helps Elizabeth. Douglas had asked him to be a pallbearer.

"Well, that pretty much says it all," I replied to my cousin.

"Yeah. Pretty much says it all. Course when you think about it, you might figure that more black folks would have showed up."

"Some did, and a lot of them came to comfort him when his daddy died."

"Yeah, but hell, you'd think more would have come, considering all he did."

"Times change," I said. I didn't want to give anyone the satisfaction of thinking I was disappointed. But I was.

At the graveside, after the service, the stories began. The preacher told the first one. It was about an incident in another café in town, this one owned by our cousin Elizabeth and her husband, Pee Wee Davis:

"One time Douglas and I were having coffee at the cafe when Elizabeth came in, and man, she was mad at Pee Wee. 'That Pee Wee Davis,' she said, tightening her lips, 'I've got all this work to do today, and he was supposed to be here getting the kitchen ready for lunch. And where is he, where is he?' Douglas started to say something but Elizabeth just cut him off. 'Now Douglas, don't you try to make excuses for your friend. I know he's off somewhere looking at a bird dog or some worthless thing like that. And I know he's gonna come in here and apologize. I swear if he says, 'Aw Honey, I just overslept, I'm sorry,' I'll just slap the fire out of him.'"

The preacher paused long enough to let some other people get closer to our group and also to make us wait a few beats. He smiled and shook his head and said, "Well sure enough, here comes old Pee Wee looking all hangdog. How you doing, Pee Wee?' Douglas asked him. 'Aw things are gonna be bad at my house, son. I was supposed to be here early and I forgot till just a few minutes ago.'"

Like all Southern story-tellers, the preacher paused again. He took his pocketknife and cut a twig off a black gum tree and stuck it in the corner of his mouth.

"Well, old Douglas just looked at Pee Wee, as if he was entirely sympathetic, and said, Pee Wee, if I was you, I'd just march back to that kitchen and say, 'Honey, I just overslept. I am so sorry and I want to make it up to you.'"

At that point we began to laugh. The preacher let it die a little, then delivered the ending, "Well, old Pee Wee went back there and told Elizabeth exactly what Douglas had told him." Another long pause then he exploded the last sentence in a great laughing voice, "And she slapped the fire out of Pee Wee. Course, by then, Douglas was out the front door."

After the laughing died down a bit, someone said, "Just like Douglas. He got a kick out of stuff like that."

There were other stories, mostly funny, about Douglas' sense of humor and his practical jokes. Elizabeth even got into the spirit. "You know, before he died," she said, "he voted an absentee ballot."

"Is that legal?"

"Absolutely. If it's voted properly it counts."

"Just like him."

Then Elizabeth said, "Douglas said he wanted to get just one more shot at those right-wingers."

Even the preacher laughed.

EPILOGUE

~

While interviewing Becky for this story, I told her that I had been disappointed that more blacks had not come to the funeral. She shrugged.

"You know," she said, "that I went to the high school when it was eighty-five percent black. I went to the prom, graduated and all that along with the black students. We were friends the same way any high school kids are friends. But I've never been invited to a class reunion."

"Really? Why? Have you contacted any of them?"

"Of course. I used to hear about the reunions and call and tell them I didn't get an invitation. They'd apologize. But I never got one so I gave up."

"Are you angry about it?"

"I used to feel hurt, but then I realized that I'm just not on their radar screen now. I've moved away and lost touch and all that."

"But that doesn't explain it.," I said, feeling a little incensed on her behalf. "After all you went through together, you deserve to go to your class reunions."

She looked at me and shook her head, her eyes reminding me of Douglas.

"It's okay," she said. "Times change. Everyone forgets."

ACKNOWLEDGMENTS

~

It is difficult to tell a story that should have been told forty-five years ago, and it would have been impossible without the help of several people who shared their memories and, indeed, their part of this story. I must include, of course, Douglas Autry's wife Elizabeth, who was shunned by many in her community, and his daughter Becky, who faced hostile students in school. Bless them both.

Also, several people who lived through those difficult days of racial turmoil and who either knew or worked with Douglas gave me invaluable information or shared their part of the story. Among them were Willie Ruth Daugherty, the Rev. William Kemp, Spence Richard, Glossie Terry, and Walter Webber.

And special thanks to my wife, Sally Pederson, who was as always encouraging and supportive throughout my research and writing.

 James A. Autry is the author
of fifteen books, the most recent of which was *On
Paying Attention; New And Selected Poems.* A former
Fortune 500 executive and magazine editor, he took
early retirement in 1991 and since then has been
writing, lecturing and conducting workshops on
Servant Leadership in this country and internationally.
He has consulted on leadership for such companies
as Starbucks, Whole Foods, New Hope Media, and
others. He helped establish a Servant Leadership
Academy in the Netherlands. For one academic year,
he held an endowed chair in leadership at Iowa State
University, and holds four honorary degrees.

The Ice Cube Press began publishing in 1991 to focus on how to live with the natural world and to better understand how people can best live together in the communities they share and inhabit. Using the literary arts to explore life and experiences in the heartland of the United States we have been recognized by a number of well-known writers including: Bill Bradley, Gary Snyder, Gene Logsdon, Wes Jackson, Patricia Hampl, Greg Brown, Jim Harrison, Annie Dillard, Ken Burns, Roz Chast, Jane Hamilton, Daniel Menaker, Kathleen Norris, Janisse Ray, Craig Lesley, Alison Deming, Harriet Lerner, Richard Lynn Stegner, Richard Rhodes, Michael Pollan, David Abram, David Orr, and Barry Lopez. We've published a number of well-known authors including: Mary Swander, Jim Heynen, Mary Pipher, Bill Holm, Connie Mutel, John T. Price, Carol Bly, Marvin Bell, Debra Marquart, Ted Kooser, Stephanie Mills, Bill McKibben, Craig Lesley, Elizabeth McCracken, Derrick Jensen, Dean Bakopoulos, Rick Bass, Linda Hogan, Pam Houston, and Paul Gruchow. Check out Ice Cube Press books on our web site, join our email list, Facebook group, or follow us on Twitter. Visit booksellers, museum shops, or any place you can find good books and support true honest to goodness independent publishing projects so you can discover why we continue striving to "hear the other side."

Ice Cube Press, LLC (Est. 1991)
North Liberty, Iowa, Midwest, USA
Resting above the Silurian and Jordan aquifers
steve@icecubepress.com
check us out on twitter and facebook
www.icecubepress.com

To Fenna Marie, the all-time "GK"!
going forward and being beautiful inside and out.

To Ingrid, my deep love, and who
flies with butterflies and ravens.